ISBN 978-1-333-81262-1
PIBN 10580295

1 MONTH OF
FREE
READING

at
www.ForgottenBooks.com

By purchasing this book you are eligible for one month membership to ForgottenBooks.com, giving you unlimited access to our entire collection of over 1,000,000 titles via our web site and mobile apps.

To claim your free month visit:

www.forgottenbooks.com/free580295

English
Français
Deutsche
Italiano
Español
Português

www.forgottenbooks.com

Mythology Photography **Fiction**
Fishing Christianity **Art** Cooking
Essays Buddhism Freemasonry
Medicine **Biology** Music **Ancient
Egypt** Evolution Carpentry Physics
Dance Geology **Mathematics** Fitness
Shakespeare **Folklore** Yoga Marketing
Confidence Immortality Biographies
Poetry **Psychology** Witchcraft
Electronics Chemistry History **Law**
Accounting **Philosophy** Anthropology
Alchemy Drama Quantum Mechanics
Atheism Sexual Health **Ancient History**
Entrepreneurship Languages Sport
Paleontology Needlework Islam
Metaphysics Investment Archaeology
Parenting Statistics Criminology
Motivational

THE

Homœopathic Law of Similarity.

AN OPEN LETTER

—TO—

Professor Justus Baron v. Liebig,

—BY—

DR. VON GRAUVOGL.

Translated from the German

— BY —

GEO. E. SHIPMAN, M. D.

———{o}———

CHICAGO:

FOUNDLINGS' HOME PRINT.

1879.

Translator's Preface.

————:o:————

WHEN the following work of von Grauvogl fell into my hands, I felt it both a duty and a privilege to give it to the English reader. The adherents of Homœopathy will read it with pleasure, as being a clear and forcible statement and defense of the Homœopathic system, while his opponents should read it, that they may see how fallacious are the objections which they make to that system. As the gifted author's pen is laid down forever, it seemed all the more desirable that what he would say, if living, to both friend and foe, should be circulated as widely as possible.

The author uses a few words which, if not peculiar to him, are not in common use and may not be intelligible to all. These are, *Hylotopics*, pertaining to the location of matter; *Hylometric*, pertaining to its measure; *Hyloteretic*, indicating the substitution of one substance for another, and *Metabolic*, the change of matter.

As in the translation of Grauvogl's Text-Book, so in this translation, I have had the kind assistance of Dr. Emil Tietze, of Philadelphia, to whom I cheerfully accord all the merits of the translation, if any are found.

In the hope that the cause of true science may be advanced by the perusal of these pages, they are given to the public.

THE TRANSLATOR.

PREFACE.

——:o:——

As in " Den Grundgesetzen der Physiologie, Pathologie und Homœ-opathischen Therapie," published last year, whose object was to strike abalance with the other curative methods, many things were but briefly treated, according as they were dependent upon other subjects, or interwoven with them, so the law of similia, even, was only considered in its significance as a guiding principle.

Hence, the following pages may serve as a complement of that work, while a public attack upon homœopathy is the cause of their appearance as a monograph.

What adherent of Hahnemann would ever tire in the effort of making the truths of homœopathy clear to his opponents?

My success in this direction has seemed to me, for a long time, like a stone thrown into the sea; it caused a bubbling motion, with a circular ripple, gradually extending, but, at the same time growing fainter and fainter, and, while these ripples were soon lost again in the sea of prejudices, the stone had also sunk in the abyss of oblivion.

I finally discovered the cause of the one phenomenon in the proverb, "*velle non discitur;*" that of the other in the labor with which the attainment of all knowledge is connected, and, that, to overcome these two hindrances it is necessary, above all, to strip of its claim the most sensitive side of our adversaries; *i. e.*, their high opinion of themselves.

To the accomplishment of this purpose I will no longer neglect any opportunity, until homœopathy has attained that position which, *in the interest of the public,* is its due.

Let the Gartenlaube and Romberg's Wissenschaften im neun-
zehnten Jahrhundert, and such *popular* writings, labor to prejudice
their readers against homœopathy as much as they please, and let
their readers, themselves, find pleasure therein : that is all a matter of
taste, and does not, in the least, affect homœopathy as a science.

When, however, men of distinction, coryphæi of science, in their
own *scientific* works, express unfavorable, and even injurious, opinions
about homœopathy, I can not refrain from giving a complete refutation of them without being treasonable to truth.

NUREMBERG, 1861.   THE AUTHOR.

An Open Letter

—TO—

Professor and Doctor Justus Baron von Liebig, etc.

—‡o‡—

BARON : In the last edition of your Chemical Letters (vol. 1, letter 4, p. 105) you have seen proper to make the following assertion :

"Who can affirm that the majority of the intelligent and educated men, of our day, show any higher degree of knowledge of Nature and its forces than the Iatro-chemists of the sixteenth century, if he knows that hundreds of physicians, educated at our universities, hold, as true, *principles which mock all experience and sound reason :* men who believe that the effects of drugs lie in certain forces or qualities which may be set in motion and increased by trituration and shaking, and can be transferred to inert substances ; who believe *that a law of Nature, which has no exception, is untrue as regards drugs, assuming, as they do, that the efficiency of drugs may be made to increase by their attenuation and by the abstraction of their efficient substance?* Surely, one would be led to think that, among the sciences which have for their object the knowledge of Nature and its forces, medicine, as an *inductive science,* has taken the lowest position."

With these assertions you throw down the gauntlet to homœopathy, and I take it up.

As President of the Royal Bavarian Academy of Sciences, you must certainly have been reminded, by your philosophic studies, that, in order to form conclusions, upon any subject, we must first determine in which category the given ideas and the conceptions of it may be combined into a unit of perception,—a cognition.

The momenta of these categories, however, the fundamental ideas of mathematical speculative philosophy, are four in number,—those of Quantity, Quality, Relation and Modality.

But your charge touching the belief that the efficiency of drugs may be made to increase by their attenuation and a decrease of their effective substance, is based only upon the one momentum of *Quantity*, as understood by physiological medicine.

Yet every substance,—hence every drug, aside from the various ponderable and imponderable quantities by which it occupies space in time,—possesses also different specific properties, or forces, according to the momentum of *Quality*. Furthermore, according to the momentum of *Modality*, the existence of any substance of this earth would be impossible, if it did not stand, with its quantities and qualities, in some proportion,—*i. e.*, *Relation*,—to other substances, and, hence, the question is as to the law according to which drugs, and their forces, must be brought into reciprocal action with the *substances and forces of the organism.*

Hence, all these momenta must be carefully considered in order to form a conclusion as to the connection of any substance of the outer world,—hence of any drug,—with our organism: without this the conclusion is one-sided,—hence, false.

This will, at once, become clear, if, for the time being, I leave the conclusion, as an abstract idea, and proceed to facts which will confirm what has been said.

That the efficiency of drugs actually increases with their attenuation, hence, with the decrease in weight of their efficient substance, has been proven, by two celebrated Professors of Physics.

First, Dr. Doppler, Professor of Physics in Prague (See Lehrbuch der physiologischen Pharmakodynamik, von Dr. Altschul), among other matters, expresses himself, on this subject, as follows:

"In fact, it can not be at all denied, that, in determining the magnitude of a great number of effects, the *weight* furnishes a very appropriate and convenient measure, and this is especially the case as regards all the effects of masses. But it is very clear that he would go too far who should assume that the units of weight suffice to indicate the mode of action of all bodies. Even the effects of frictional electricity must be determined by quite other units than those of *weight*, not to mention many other natural phenomena.

"Hence, before we may feel at liberty to pronounce something as large or small, or, even, on account of its supposed insignificance, to dismiss it to the realm of chimeras, we must, as it seems to me, first of all, have demonstrated and established the *unit* which is to be its assumed base, in order to determine whether, in judging of the same, we must use the balance or the foot-rule.

" In due consideration of these facts, I propose, for the sake of an example, the following question : By what right do we determine the effect of drugs by their weight, and not, rather, by the size of their efficient *superficies;* or, in other words, is it the inner or the outer part of a drug which, being brought into contact with the world of sensation, produces its drug action ?"

" By the physical surface of a body, in contradistinction to its mathematical, we comprise the sum of all those bodily atoms which, in one direction, at least, are surrounded by atoms of another kind. Hence it follows, at once, that bodies which are broken up or in any way reduced in size, must gain much in surface, since the atoms which were previously within the body now come in contact with the adjacent menstruum and, consequently, form a part of the new surface. But it is just as clear, on the contrary, that two or more bodies of the same kind, which formerly constituted a unit, or which otherwise fit closely together, if they are joined together, must each lose its surface, at least, at the points of contact, since the idea of an intervening space must be abandoned. A more close consideration of this subject leads us, further, to the conclusion that the total superficies *increases* in, at least, the same—and generally in a much greater—ratio, as the diameters of the separate particles *diminish.*

" Hence, for example, if a cubic inch of any substance is reduced to particles of the size of coarse sand, forming thus more than a million of separate particles, its surface has then *increased* already, as a very easy calculation will show, to about six or seven square feet. Again, microscopic investigations show us that particles of slacked lime, flour, and many other pulverulent bodies which Nature and Art often present us, while still visible to the naked eye, are a hundred times smaller than the grain of sand just mentioned. Hence, if we triturate the above-mentioned quantity of a substance — a cubic inch — to such a fineness as just stated, the total superficies presents an area of more than *one thousand square feet.*

" But, in order that this surface should really present itself as a physical or active one, we must, at the very start, seek to prevent these separate particles from coming in contact with each other, which, as it seems to me, can hardly be accomplished in any other way than by mixing the drug in question, at the beginning of the process, with some foreign body,—sugar of milk, for instance,—as a vehicle, and by simultaneously triturating the two together. The *menstruum*, or vehicle, must be added in sufficient quantity."

Will you have the goodness to show the falsity of these statements (if you intend to maintain the above-cited charge against homœopathy)? for they perfectly establish, according to natural law, the efficiency of homœopathic triturations, in opposition to your opinion.

This law of surface-action is apparent in porous bodies, even within their very volume, without the necessity of reducing the same.

In the text-book of Dr. Schultze, in Greifswalde for instance, we find that "wood, as its vegetable fibre does not melt, furnishes charcoal, of a dull appearance, possessing entirely the organic texture of the wood, as one can satisfy himself, by the external appearance, and, still better, by examining fine sections thereof under the microscope. Owing to this cellular structure, a surface proportionately very large is obtained, within a space very small. If each cell, under a proper light, has a diameter of $\frac{1}{1500}$ of an inch, and, if we assume that the thickness of the walls is one-third of the diameter of the cells, then, a square inch would contain 1,000,000, and a cubic inch, 1,000,000,000 cells; but the walls of each cell, supposing it to be cubic, has a superficies of $6 \times \frac{1}{2,250,000}$ of a square inch; hence, the sum of the walls of all the cells contained in a cubic inch of wood, or charcoal, are $\frac{6,000,000,000}{2,250,000}$, equal to 2,666 square inches, which equal 18 square feet. The *mechanical power of attraction*, which the surface of the coal has, in reference to gaseous and fluid substances, or solid substances in a state of solution, is, it is true, first of all, dependent upon the specific peculiarity of this surface (a dull surface is more efficient than a smooth, shining, one); but, notwithstanding that, however, it is chiefly sustained by the extent of this surface. Hence, if so large a surface is concentrated in so small a volume, as in the case of charcoal, it can not surprise us that that superficies, whenever the force of attraction decides, *accomplishes much more than an equal volume, or weight, of a coal of solid and vesicular texture.*

"Many other porous bodies resemble charcoal in this respect. One cubic inch of platina black, for example, takes up 253,440 cubic inches of oxygen. It has been calculated that a cubic inch of this preparation of platina possesses a surface of 200,000 square feet."

I present these observations, taken from inorganic Nature, under the law of the surface-action, merely for the reason that, in the human organism, there is actually not a single solid body,—not a single com-pact molecule,—to be found. The very bones have a cellular struc-ture, which is not lost, even on incineration, on which account the os-seous carbon rivals wood charcoal in the power of absorbing gaseous and fluid bodies,—an indisputable proof that nothing within the or-ganism can be judged merely according to the momentum of quantity, weight, size, or volume.

As regards homœopathic *attenuations*, permit me now to quote to you a few words from Dr. Jolly, Professor of Physics at Munich, as found in his pamphlet, entitled "Ueber die Physik der Molecular-kræfte," 1857. He there repeats the declaration of Copernicus, "that all appearances may be against his assertion," but that he has proved, by experiment and observation, "that the molecular attraction be-tween the molecules of a solvent and those of a dissolved substance, causes an *approximation* of the molecules, hence a contraction; that an *addition of the solvent increases the sphere of the action of every mole-cule of the dissolved substance.*"

This action of the molecules he followed up in a 12 per cent solution of saltpetre, prepared in 1,000 C.C. of water, and calculated that, after having attenuated the same solution with 28,633.3 C.C. of water, a still further contraction of this solution, amounting to 13 C.C., took place; an action of the saltpetre molecules, in this *strong attenuation*, equal to the pressure of eight atmospheres, as will be set forth in §§ 78, 79, and 80.

If you can not refute these experiments of Professor Jolly, then your charge against homœopathic attenuations, which are prepared in an analogous manner, is refuted.

If, however, you are not inclined to lend an ear to physics, and de-mand the proof against your assertions from chemistry, I only need mention that chemical combinations are the least apt to occur between solid bodies; more readily between fluids, and most readily between gaseous bodies; that Professors Kirchhoff and Bunsen forcibly blew three milligrammes—about one-half a grain—of chloride of soda, with sugar of milk, into a room, which contained about 60 C. M. of air; that, in a few minutes, soda-lines presented themselves, in the flame, standing at a distance; that, consequently, this one-half grain had been separated into an immense molecular surface, in such a manner that the naked eye could perceive, with the greatest clearness, less than a trillionth of a milligramme of this salt.

Here, accordingly, an *effect* "was produced with the decrease and attenuation of the efficient substance," in which chemistry, till now, has *never* believed; an effect which will finally accustom even our *learned adversaries* to the figures of homœopathic attenuations. By such experiments, taught in their own laboratories, our opponents will soon find themselves in the footsteps of homœopathy, and will no longer be able to withhold from it their approval and admiration; for spectral analysis has opened, even to chemical inquiry, a territory heretofore closed, reaching beyond the ends of the earth,— yes, even beyond the confines of the solar system. Even in the atmosphere, the soda reaction is rarely absent, though no chemist ever had an inkling thereof. Nevertheless, the absence, or presence, of such minimal, but widely diffused, quantities of common salt, in our atmosphere, must have the greatest influence upon man,— the child of the earth,— and no one will doubt it.

Not to dwell too long upon this subject, to which I refer again, in ? 81, I must, moreover, present to you some evidences, from organic life, in favor of these experiments.

The great efficiency of infinitely small molecules, hitherto beyond the reach of chemistry, is fully confirmed by the experiments with human milk, given in ?? 34 and 41.

The experiments of Hodgkin also show how powerfully imponderable quantities penetrate the organism. He laid a compress upon each arm of a man, and moistened one with a solution of hydriodate of potash, and the other with a solution of starch. He then closed the the galvanic current, connected with these two points, whereupon the starch was colored blue. Hence, the hydriodate must have been decomposed, and passed through the body in imponderable quantities.

Prof. Schmidt, in Dorpat, found that arsenic, in the smallest dose, produces a diminution in the metamorphosis of tissue, amounting to from 20 to 40 per cent, because it depresses the excretion of carbonic acid and urea, so decidedly that an equivalent quantity of fat and albumen remains in the system, and the *weight* and *fullness* of the body are increased; and, yet, to speak of it in passing, the popular idea of "poison," is deemed, at the universities, a scientific one, though arsenic-eaters, who begin at the age of 18 years, with a dose of arsenious acid, the size of a millet seed, subsequently consume 2, 4, and even 5, grains at a dose, and yet live to be 70 years old. (Chem. Centr.-Blatt 20, 1861.)

Or, can yon explain the great results produced during *growth*, and in the nutrition of man, otherwise than by the law of diosmosis, and the peculiarity of the membranous structures of our bodies, to allow fluids to pass the more readily the more they are *attenuated*.

Could you be ignorant of the effects of imponderable quantities of vaccine virus, which are not any less surprising, and which continue so long that they do not make their appearance till eight days after vaccination, and, then, in addition, produce violént fever, swelling of the arm, and a luxurious vesicular eruption?

If, in the face of these facts, you should still be unable to comprehend the great efficiency of minute doses of drugs, or if you should wish still other examples of the greater efficiency of small quantities of substances in organisms,—an efficiency greater in proportion to that considerable less efficiency of their larger masses,—the pearl oyster, in § 75, presents a striking example. Investigations, also, like those of Dr. Mosthoff, belong here. He made many experiments, with various attenuations of Hyoscyamine, which presented results that will, most surely, surprise you, since, while a drop of the first attenuation produced no effect, upon the human eye, after the use of the same substance, in the sixth attenuation, a great dilatation of the pupils was manifest.

I can, moreover, present you examples against your assertion from the therapeutics of men of your own faith, even. Thus, I learned, personally, many years ago, in Ischl, from the celebrated balneo-therapeutist, Dr. Brenner v. Felsach, that five measures of common salt produced far more effect in 1,000 measures of water, than when the baths were more strongly saturated with it.

If, to such facts, I add the contents of §§ 77, 82 and 90, it is no part of my intention to weary you with the narration of many others, which demonstrate the great effects of the smallest molecules, and the increase of the efficiency of substances with the decrease of their ponderable masses, in which Nature is so rich, and of which natural science daily makes new discoveries.

Had you thought of all this before you conceived your attacks against homœopathy, you would have seen that, with that charge, you have even contradicted yourself, which may be readily demonstrated by evidence from the latest edition of your Chemical Letters.

In volume II, page 119, for instance, you write: "The effect of free hydrochloric acid, upon the plastic constituents of the food, is very remarkable. Gluten of cereals and animal fibrin dissolve readily and rapidly, in the temperature of the body, in water which is barely acidulated, and this solubility *does not increase, but decreases*, when the quantity of acid in the fluid is *increased*, so that all which is dissolved may be precipitated again, by hydrochloric acid moderately concen-

trated. A solution of common salt acts in a similar way. The very
water, which, by an addition of .001 of hydrochloric acid, becomes a
powerful solvent, for the above-mentioned plastic constituents, *loses*
its solvent power when it contains more than 3 per cent of common
salt, and, from an acid solution of gluten or animal fibrin, every thing
which is dissolved may be separated again by a solution of common
salt."

If you needed, hence, a thousand-fold attenuation of free hydrochloric acid, for the solution of gluten and animal fibrin, you could
not seriously maintain, in the spirit of your attack against homœopathy, that the more hydrochloric acid you used the more gluten and
animal fibrin you could dissolve. On the contrary, you must, *invita
ope*, according to homœopathy, *potentize*, as did Hahnemann, with his
drugs, the free hydrochloric acid, in order to gain the effect just
mentioned.

How far such attenuations must go for organisms, *you, yourself, show,*
on page 295 of the same volume, where you explain the matter, as follows: "The richest manuring with earthy phosphates, in a coarse
powder, can scarcely be compared, in its effect, with a far smaller
quantity in an *infinite state of subdivision*, which has the result that a
particle of the phosphate is found in every part of the land. A single
root-fibre requires *infinitely little* for its nourishment, from the spot
where it touches the soil, but it is necessary, for its function and sub-
sistence, that this *minute* quantity should be present just at that very
spot, for if the nutritious substances do not dissolve in water, then an
excess in every other part of the field is of no avail for the nourishment of that root-fibre.

Now—homœopathy, likewise, meets the very same experience in
the human organism, to-wit: that drugs must be so triturated, attenuated, and transferred to inert bodies,— suspended, for instance,— or
dissolved in water or alcohol, that they become smaller than the cali-
bres of the capillary vessels, in order to be taken up by these radicles
of our nutrition; and, indeed, that they *must be infinitely smaller* than
the blood corpuscle, which, itself, is composed of a number of differ
ent substances. §§ 40, 75.

You present still many other evidences, in your Chemical Letters,
which prove that your own experiments overthrow your charge against
homœopathy; the above, however, may suffice to call your attention
to the others.

If I enter upon the fundamental reasons which caused homœopathy to adopt the principle against which you contend, the variety of these few examples clearly point to them, and you, yourself, must acknowledge, that, in conceiving your attack upon homœopathy, you left entirely out of view the categories of *modality* and *relation*, for, if you had thought of them, you would have, as remarked in ₰ 28, appreciated the difference between *cause* and *condition*, without which one might, even, maintain that the sun was the only cause of day.

Evidently, you have, yourself, no clear idea of that "*increasing*" in the efficiency of drugs by their dilution and decrease of efficient substance, maintained by homœopathy, since, with those words, only a relation of quantity is expressed, in a general manner, without thus, however, defining of what kind this relation is. Moreover, you consider this "increasing" merely as an established phenomenon, and recognize but your own views about it—a proceeding that can not be without self-deception. For this word—this "increasing"—supplies the place of very different relations of objective facts, which can not be obtained by abstract thought, and, consequently, should have been expressed in the conclusion.

Homœopathy, it can not be denied, maintained, in a general way, and when it was, itself, only an empiricism, that drugs should increase in efficiency by their attenuation, and you maintain the same thing, *in form*, though conversely.

But both affirmations are void, *per se*, for in neither are the *qualitative* changes considered, which, on one hand, are *produced* by such attenuations, in various *substances*, while, on the other, there is no mention made of the material conditions of the organism under which the effect of those changed substances may, and does, follow.

A single example, however, will lead us very quickly to an understanding of this matter :

Physiological medicine knows, for instance, no other effect of colocynth than the drastic ; at the most, an experiment has been made, here and there, to ascertain whether it might be used, also, as a diuretic or an emmenagogue.

Now, homœopathy has never maintained that the action of colocynth, in the *third attenuation*,— that is to say, by the way, in the trillionth parts of half a grain,—is, likewise, confined, locally, to the intestinal canal, or that it is more drastic than any of its ponderable quantities ; but it did, and does yet, maintain that the action of colocynth, by its attenuation, enters into mutual action with the whole organism, and, only on this ground, specifically increases in its reach, but not at all in *intensity* as a *drastic;* that colocynth, in its third attenuation, of course, would no longer produce *diarrhœa;* but, on the contrary, would gain a *greater sphere of operation*, and, in consequence thereof, cure not only a specific form of diarrhœa, arising from other causes, but also cases of dysentery, ischias, asthma, etc.— an assertion which can be verified, any day, at the bedside.

The processes of such cures are quite analogous with those of spectral analysis ; for, according to experiments and observations, made at the bedside, the remedies, in their attenuations,—just like that very high attenuation of common salt blown into the room by Bunsen and Kirchhoff,—attain, within the organism, to such an expansion, that, provided they meet a pathological locality, suitable to their sphere of operation,— analogous to the flame, in the other case,— they very promptly make themselves known, by the relief of suffering, which they produce,—just as the microscopically divided salt made itself known, by those spectral lines,—no matter how distant the point of application was from the point of reception into the organism.

Since, further, these experiments and observations, to-wit.: the homœopathic drug provings, have established the various spheres and manners of operation of these drugs, in their mutual action with the organism, as will appear from the following paragraphs, thus every new attempt at a cure confirms the truth of the indications correctly drawn from them, just as every new experiment with the spectral analysis, confirms the former, only that the conditions for the latter are far easier to fulfill than the establishment of those indications. But whenever the homœopathic drug reaches no pathological localities corresponding to it, then it is quite without effect, just as the minutely divided salt is, without the flame.

Hence, these homœopathic attenuations can no more produce or increase the effects of their *ponderable* quantities, than the common salt, in its attenuation, in the spectral analysis, can crystalize into octaedra, or, boiled with sulphate of magnesia, form Glauber's salts.

Many errors of thought and judgment arise from an apparent meaning which renders a conclusion ambiguous, for the reason that it is based upon relative conceptions,—upon ideas which do not have their origin in experience, and have no objective substratum, but express only a relation of an object to an idea,—conceptions, of which, however, empiricism very often, and involuntarily, avails itself.

Such ideas contain no predicate, but only relations, such as similar, opposite, various, to decrease, to increase, to be finite, infinite, etc.

You have thus, I admit, with your assertion that the effect of drugs can not increase with the decrease of their efficient substance, expressed a relation, but you have not been able to master the source of your inference, and have determined the possible and actual merely according to the rule of comparative ideas. But the existence of things is not settled by the manner in which I am accidentally able to understand it. On the contrary, I have to comprehend things as they actually are. To gain conviction, in this way, you have neglected.

Has it not happened to you, as it has to those who affirm that the world is finite, because nothing can be without beginning and end, or as it occurred to others, who affirm that the world is infinite, because time and space, in which it exists, are infinite? for each of these two parties judges the world under the supposition that it is just that which each understands it to be. Clearly, both these assertions must be false, for there is yet a third case, viz: that the world does not stand, and never stood a moment, under the law of quantity.

Instead of correcting the error in that inexact generalizing conclusion of empirical homœopathy, you have simply denied it, and, hence, have placed yourself upon the same level with it, for particularly affirmative opinions possess, conversely, the same worth and the same value.

If you had also considered that before, and had gone to the bottom of the matter, before you had determined to indite your assault upon homœopathy, you would have further discovered that the *law of nature* to which you alluded, to-wit: that of *causality*, is *not* the law of the organism, and that it can not be appealed to for events which stand to each other in the relation of simultaneousness. For the cause determines the effect, according to the law of causality, it is a relation of *succession*, as a more heavy clap of thunder follows a more powerful streak of lightning, or as one blow upon a nail will drive it less deeply into some soft substance than two of equal force. In such events, with the effect, the end thereof is also always given, or, by continning causes, the effect, indeed, reaches further, but only in the *same* direction, in the same way and manner.

According to the law of *reciprocal action*, however, which is the law of the organism, a cause determines not merely a single result, in one direction, but the result, itself, determines again another cause, *quite different* from the former, so that mutual dependences take place.

Arsenic, for example, even in the smallest dose, produces not only a
diminution of the metamorphosis of tissue, but will, if given contin-
uously, be the cause of quite other phenomena, as is well known.
Even outside of the human organism, the same difference exists between the dependence and co-existence of phenomena, which results
from every experiment.

The organism is a system of outer actions and counter-actions,
which take place automatically, according to the mechanical laws of
reciprocal action, and in opposition to that of a machine, which possesses no automatic counter-actions, but only causes and momenta of
inertia, to be overcome by the former; in contradistinction, moreover,
to the counter-actions of inorganic bodies, produced by technic manip-
ulations, which take place, for example, in chemical combinations.
While here, after the chemical combination has been completed by the
production of a new body, all action and counter-action ceases, and
this body can never automatically begin anew the motions from which
it originated; furthermore, while the machine, after the removal of
its motor cause, or by virtue of a cause aiming at a change of one of
its motions, at once, stands still, or is broken,—a motion in the organism, changed by a cause which does not make it sick, or destroy it, returns automatically to its previous form, according to its own laws,
as soon as this cause has ceased to act; for example, not every thing
stands still, in the organism, under the action of some narcotic substance, and whatever this substance has caused to rest, for a time, returns, automatically, to its specific function, as soon as the narcosis
has expended itself.

This happens, also, by virtue of a cause which made the organism
sick, if the conditions for the possibility of that influence, or of its
continuance, are removed by the physician.

In the place of such organic laws, the term "vital force" is used,
by teachers of natural sciences, to express the difference between organic and inorganic bodies; but the *practical physician* would know as
little what to do with this idea as with the idea of "poison," hence
his knowledge must go deeper, he must dispense with all ideas which
conceal facts, and search for different laws of Nature, which actually
lie at the bottom of the phenomena, from the superficial observation
of which such collective ideas were gathered.

As regards your proposition as to the use of the inductive conclusion, I request you to bear in mind that this can be applied only on the
strength of *experiment and observation.*

As a proof of this, I shall present two striking examples, from which you can not fail, at once, to perceive that your own technical instruments,—your chemical re-agents,—are very far from offering you the security for which you trust them, in your attack upon homœopathy, since they do not always suffice, even, in the domain of your own science.

Chemistry, long ago, found quantities of phosphoric acid in the seeds of cereals, quite considerable in proportion, while it could discover none in the ground, or only here and there the merest trace. Could we now deny that the seeds of these plants took up phosphoric acid from the soil upon which they grew, on the strength of these negative experiments? At any rate, such a negation would contain no inductive conclusion. It is only later times that have shed light upon this question, since chemistry has really discovered, in almost all sorts of soil and rocks, *small quantities* of phosphoric acid, which plants have been taking up from the same soil, for thousands of years, and concentrating in their seeds.

Kirchhoff and Bunsen have, also, lately demonstrated, by their spectro-analytical observations, the existence of two *entirely new* alkaline metals, which may be found at the Sool-springs, at Kreuznach and Duerkheimer, and in the thermal spring, Ungemach, at Baden-Baden, while the best chemists and analysts never could discover them with their re-agents. Should those analysts maintain that this could not be possible, since they never found these alkaline metals in these springs, then they, also, would venture an arbitrary, but not an inductive, conclusion.

Hence, it can not be *at all allowed* to maintain the non-existence or inefficiency of a body, and its forces, because it is *so very attenuated* in its solution, that chemistry can not discern it; for all these conclusions lack the necessary premises, to-wit: experience, on account of inadequate experiments and observations.

Moreover, you have overlooked the fundamental principle, that all inductive experiences can be drawn only from positive experiments and observations, and, hence, could not satisfy the requirements necessary to the formation of an inductive conclusion regarding the mode of action of homœopathic drugs, since you never have deemed it necessary to institute investigations according to the dictates of homœopathy, as a practical physician or a clinician, or to allow others to make them.

2

Hence, in the method of your attack against homœopathy, you have *not proceeded inductively.* You will, however, learn, in the following pages, the inductive conclusions of homœopathy.

In view of all these numerous arguments against you, *based upon indisputable facts,* I can not err very much if I affirm that your attack upon homœopathy, scattered all over the world, is a *phantom, which lacks any and every scientific basis,* and reduces itself, under the most charitable construction, into arbitrary ideas, void of all value, entertained only by those illy informed.

But this is not the most important result which can be drawn from your attack.

The great force of your attack lies in the high position to which you have attained in the world, and which accounts for the fact that you have the great majority of learned men, as a chorus, sing as you will.

In fact, you may find your attack already copied, almost *verbatim,* as a *quos ego* against homœopathy, in medical works.

Since, now, from the foregoing refutation of your attack upon homœopathy, it appears, beyond a doubt, that you lack any and every experience regarding what homœopathy is, I take the liberty of presenting you, in the subsequent pages, a small sketch of its nature, thus giving you an opportunity to find other errors, in homœopathy, which defy experience and a sound understanding.

The last motive which inclined me to venture upon this undertaking is this: that, then, I might, probably, hope that you would maturely consider what homœopathy is, before arrogating to yourself, and presenting to the public, opinions upon subjects which you are not accustomed seriously to consider.

The result of this consideration can terminate in but one of two possibilities: Either you will pronounce the doctrines and laws of Nature, according to which homœopathy proceeds, as utterly worthless,—in which case, I beg for better information, and for a refutation, conformable to the laws of philosophical criticism, and free from any individual or arbitrary opinions, of all the charges brought by me against physiological medicine; or you will acknowledge those doctrines and laws of Nature as wholly true, and reject allopathy, or the so-called physiological medicine. In the latter case, however, I beg for an immediate withdrawal of all your charges against homœopathy, and, at the same time, for the influence of your elevated and powerful position, energetically to remove all the *hindrances* to the free practice of homœopathy, wherever, and of whatever nature, they may be.

You will, finally, grant this latter request, all the more surely, as it was a ruling principle of the Royal Bavarian Academy, and, it is to be hoped, still is, to permit free inquiry into science, and to resist all *coteries* preventing such inquiry.

Having gained, for yourself, imperishable laurels, by your labors for the benefit of those in health, you will,—if you unite with me in the conviction that no enjoyment of science and art exists for the sick, whose number far exceeds that of the well,—rejoice in the opportunity of being able to labor, also, for the benefit of diseased humanity, and to dispel, finally, at any price, the painful uncertainty which distresses the public, concerning the fitness of their physicians.

NUREMBURG, 1861.   DR. V. GRAUVOGL.

INTRODUCTION.
—:o:—
§1.

"The true curative method," said Hahnemann, "is based upon the maxim: In order to cure gently, quickly, surely, and permanently, select such a drug, in each individual case of disease, as may produce an affection (*homoion pathos*) similar to that it is expected to cure (*similia similibus curantur !*)."

Thus runs Hahnemann's law of similarity, as expressed in the form of a general indication.

"This homœopathic curative method," he proceeds, "no one has heretofore taught,—no one has practised; but if the truth lies in this method, alone, as experience will readily show, then it may be expected that, though it be not acknowledged for a century, traces of it may yet be found, in all ages."

§ 2.

Hahnemann now cites a number of such examples, from Hippocrates down to his own day, which would serve to confirm the above propositions.

More than sixty years have passed; thousands of physicians have, up to this time, accepted these propositions as correct, and always have found them reliable, in their practise; yet the overwhelming majority of physicians denies them. While a single case of a properly-conducted homœopathic cure was quite enough for the majority of those physicians, who, thereby, had become adherents of Hahnemann, indelibly to impress them with the truth of these propositions, millions of such cases, presented to the opponents, only gave them occasion to dispute their truth, by every conceivable means, although—or, rather, because—they neglected to make them subjects of a careful examination.

§ 3.

It has become stale to be always drawling out, and repeating, over and over again, the old tune, that this was owing to the fact that our opponents, unconditionally, accept as true, and retail, through their lives, whatever they were made to believe in their youth; for the causes of that fact lie, partly, in the laws of our perceptive capacity, partly, I am sorry to say, in private interests, which ought to stand aloof from science, but which, notwithstanding, have fastened upon it fetters all the stronger.

With regard to skeptics, Hahnemann points to experience. We must confess, however, that with the affirmation that a certain thing *is*, it is not, at the same time, explained *why* it is, and the lack of this basis of knowledge imposes upon men, who are not accustomed to independent thought, the trouble of telling where to seek that basis.

This skeptical conduct of our adversaries, immediately changes into the opposite (credulity), as soon as one of them announces that he has found a new remedy for a disease. The "why" he has always right at hand; as, for example, he is wont to reason thus: All inflammations are dangerous diseases; nitre is a cooling salt; therefore, nitre is a remedy against those dangerous diseases. But this inference is just as erroneous as the following: All beaters* are dangerous men; Cajus is a drum-beater; therefore, Cajus is a dangerous man; for neither the objective nor essential connection of nitrum with the cure of an inflammation is contained in this inference. Such a connection is, moreover, unknown to allopathy; for, in all its so-called anti-phlogistic prescriptions, the stereotypic nitrum still appears, to this very day, the chief factor.

The subject, logically considered, stands thus: Every progressive syllogism can consist only of three ideas,— of two subjects and a general idea; but a regressive syllogism our opponents can not form, because they lack the conditions necessary for induction. If that connection were known to them, they would possess synthetic-hypothetic inferences for the formation of their inductions, which, if they are not to end in downright fallacies, must consist of three ideas, and not of four, as in that example.

This example quite suffices, as regards the general character of all the other prescriptions of physiological medicine.

---

*This is an inconvenient syllogism to translate into English. "Schlager" means a beater, a bruiser, a fighter, a boxer; but "beater" is not an English word.—*Translator.*

3

On the strength of such inferences, without hesitation, the experiment, with the favorite remedy, is made, at once, upon all patients, just as if they existed only to be experimented upon, while the experiments should have been made previously, so as, at least, to have obtained inductive inferences for the formation of the indications. If a homœopath should advise these physicians, to be guided by the laws of Nature, they would, at once, be completely nonplussed.

§ 4.

Hence, we must make it easier for these gentlemen; and, since the good of suffering humanity is at stake, we must do for them what ought to be a part of their own calling. The only difficulty lies in this : that the expression, "law of similarity," can not be further analyzed, for it consists merely of relative ideas with the copula *curantur*, the objective conceptions of which are endless.

Hence, instead of that, we will analyze the *subjects* which make up its general range, and present the nature of its meaning, according to scientific (naturo-philosophical) criticism, *i. e.*, thus explain the facts which flow from the *Simile*, or, from the law of similarity, by the existing laws of Nature, from which the significance of the simile must issue, of its own accord.

§ 5.

To solve this problem, we need, among other things, the guide of mathematical (abstract) philosophy.

However, I read, in the fourth edition (just appeared, in 1861) of the "Grundzuege der Wissenschaftlichen Botanik," by Prof. Schleiden, one of the greatest worshipers of philosophy, as the previous editions of his work show: That most of the younger men of our age have never had, even, the opportunity of learning "that there exists, in fact, a philosophy which is the highest perfection and finishing touch of scientific education, and that Hegel is related to Kant and all true philosophers about as a modern astrologer is to Newton and the astronomers." "Yet," Schleiden continues, "it is certain that there is a universal repugnance to philosophy, and, in view of the richness of the natural sciences, in special problems, at which, for a long time to come, all the gifted can try their hands, I have but little hope that the taste for philosophical studies will soon reappear in the foreground of mental evolution.

I give, now, the reasons which, apart from the necessary requirements of every science, induced me not to subject myself, and, still
less, homœopathy, to the caprice of the majority.

In the first place, Humboldt declares, in his Kosmos (p. 69), that
"science begins where the intellect takes hold of a subject,—where an
attempt is made to subject the sum of observations to the criticism of
Reason : this is the mind turned toward Nature." And, p. 71 : " Quite
recently, the mathematical part of abstract philosophy enjoyed a great
and glorious cultivation. A misuse, or faulty direction, of intellectual
labor, however, must not lead to the idea, degrading to intelligence,
that the world of thought were, according to its nature, the region of
fantastic fallacies, and that the exuberant treasures of empiricism,
gathered during so many centuries, were threatened by philosophy, as
by a hostile power."

A Humboldt, though neither he, himself, nor Schleiden, ever made
a practical use of the instruments of a mathematical abstract philosophy, might well impress that majority, and, all the more, as the quantity,—the extent of an opinion, if ever so numerously defended and
propagated,—can never give a criterion for the correctness of its quality.

§ 6.

Utterly to destroy the well-known vitality of prejudices, it is necessary to pull them up by the roots. When I am told that I have, in my
work,"Ueber den Grundgesetzen der Physiologie,Pathologie und homœ-
opathischen Therapie," chosen the weakest points of the physiological
school for my assault, for which reason it had been very easy for me to
make a breach, I reply that the former was not the case. I directed
my attack, even there, upon the premises, upon the main pillars, upon
which the whole building rests, so that structure and foundation might
all be overthrown together; and, if that task was such an easy matter,
why did no one else do it, long before me ?

Let us hear, now, from one of the leaders of that majority,—let us
hear Molleschot,—who made it his aim not to judge, but only to comprehend, empirically, with the organs of sense.

In his work, just referred to, entitled, "Kreislauf des Lebens," p.
21, we find : " Philosophizing means thinking, and knowledge means to
know facts, in the domain of nature, art and states."

You may make a layman believe that; but, in science, there is a
difference between thinking and judging, or intellectual perception;

and, in order to lay claim to the knowledge of a fact, science requires, at the same time, the knowledge of its *conditions*.

Molleschot says, p. 417: "Law is only the shortest general expression for the concordance of many thousand statements. The law has only historical value. It interprets the phenomenon; it confines the change of phenomena to a short formula; it connects the sum of the properties with a word, but it *does not govern it*.

From this, we see that Molleschot believes the numerical, statistical results to be the law. They, however, surely, never govern facts; on the contrary, for these results, the law, according to which they happen, must be first sought and found. Entangled in such confusion, he does not hesitate to remark, immediately afterward, "for thought is the living expression of the *law*.

But the matter stands thus: The excitement, through the senses, produces the *state of sensation*, upon which, afterward, by the formation of further associations, according to the law of habit, the lower, or involuntary, train of thought, resting upon memory, arises. But, above this, the self-evolution, through the intellect, takes place; *i. e.*, the higher, *voluntary*, train of thought,—the logical.

An example will make Molleschot's standpoint clear.

In order to demonstrate his favorite proposition, that, in all important discoveries, of all ages, in the domains of science, art, and mechanics, it was always a sensual observation which offered the starting point, he says, p. 405: "Biot has lately written, 'Mathematicians have a perfect knowledge of the circle, though neither nature nor art has ever shown a perfect circle.' The assertion is quite correct; but it is just as well established that man could discover the properties of the circle only by seeing the circular line in the sand; only by means of a sensual delineation of it."

Molleschot may satisfy himself, and his fellows, with such polemic artifices; but, here, again, the matter stands somewhat differently. By subjective, voluntary contemplation, it is true, I may learn to see that the diameter of a circle is to the circumference as 1 to 3.14159. What, then, connects the intellect with this necessary truth,—with this peculiarity of the circle? It can not be the nature of the circle, for I learn the nature of the circle from this knowledge. Hence, I do not gain *a posteriori*, *i. e.*, by measuring, that relation of numbers, empirically, from the perception of the circle; on the contrary, I ascribe it to every circle, *a priori*, however many circles have been, or may be, drawn. This law—these numbers of Ludolph—were, indeed, found by means of voluntary thought; but, after we possess it, it exists no longer subjectively, but *objectively*, for every one, and for all time, and as objectively as the very fact of a circle drawn in the sand, which fact, however, exists, once at a time, just as often as it is accomplished, and which may be accomplished by the drawing of innumerable sizes of circles, but never except according to the law of Ludolph's proportion, which *governs every circle*. There is a multitude of problems in mechanics, in architecture, etc., to be solved, which, without this proportion, could only be solved empirically; hence, for example, after faulty constructions had already been made, by new constructions, equally faulty, and which problems may, possibly, be solved once, and at a time which can not definitely be calculated.

By this illustration, I trust I have made the relation between law and empiric fact, between the bitterly-denounced, so-called "*a priori,*' and the adored "*a posteriori*," sufficiently apparent.

Most strangely sounds the glorification of the *a posteriori* from the lips of physicians, for whom it is impossible to establish a single indication, at the sick-bed, without the presupposition of the necessary laws for the occurrence of the results anticipated, and to be introduced by the prescription, within the organism of the patient.

The precision of conclusions, from the premises of the existing laws of Nature, is the only guarantee for the precision of results at the sick-bed.

To ascribe to this, *a priori*, another meaning would indicate a less than ordinary acquaintance with the present standpoint of the natural sciences.

Hence, it is not the existence of things that depends upon a law, but their connection; for I know, for instance, even *a priori*, that the magnet, necessarily, attracts iron; but, in order that the attraction may take place, iron must first be brought near.

A thought and a conclusion, according to natural law, to which, it must be admitted, allopathy is a stranger, since it never knows how to connect facts with their laws, can, hence, never lead to error, but must always protect therefrom.

§ 7.

Let us inquire, now, upon what presuppositions Hahnemann was able to establish his law of cure.

It was absolutely known to him from immediate observation, *i.e.* he abstracted from the whole of his knowledge, that, in the compass of his mediate perceptions, not accident, but the necessity of the laws of nature ruled. However, he thus only expressed a doctrine which it is true was always confirmed in practice, but he did not speak of the scientific sphere of its execution. He did maintain, however, that, his doctrine rested upon the assumption that a weaker dynamic affection was permanently removed, in the living, by another stronger one similar to it, and merely differing according to its nature. But, with this hypothesis, he ventured upon a field of objective facts unknown to him and his age and attempted to explain the unknown by a super-sensual mode.

On the contrary, the essence of a thing is its cause, and, since the same cause cannot remove what it produced, so, thus very evidently his drugs could not cure the same forms of disease which they produced in their provings upon the healthy, and could not produce upon the healthy the same forms of disease which they were to cure, but only similar ones, *i.e.* such as agreed, not according to the *cause* but the *form*.

Hahnemann drew this conclusion, quite correctly, from the law of causation.

§ 8.

From this follows, at the same time, that Hahnemann paid attention only to the complex of symptoms, but none to nosological names such as the school is wont to furnish, for practice taught him that these names indicated merely some ideas generalized according to this or that prominent symptom, which often led, as above remarked, to erroneous therapeutic conclusions. Besides, it cannot be a matter of indifference whether, for example, an inflammation has attacked a child or an old man, a girl or a man, and, that in consequence of *far more* different conditions, the same effect could not be expected from the same cause.

Hence Hahnemann's conclusions, viz: that diseases are unrecognizable from changes produced within, but clearly recognizable by the group of symptoms, was all the less to be found fault with in his day; for, with this proposition, he found himself again in the scheme of causality, according to which a *change* always pre-supposes a cause, which changes an object into a condition, which is contradictorily opposed to its former condition. This would, hence, be a contrarium in the final effect resulting from the indication according to the *simile*.

Owing to reasons which controlled his time he had to refuse further investigation into the How of this final effect.

§ 9.

Instead of that, however, he stood immovable upon his assertion that the groups of morbid symptoms, which drugs produce iu *healthy* men are the only object from which we can learn their curative power in disease. With this proposition, Hahnemann evidently rests upon the laws of the organism and expresses, moreover, the postulate resting upon those laws — the postulate of a comparison between two *objects*, between the *whole* of a group of symptoms belonging to a disease *artificially* produced on the healthy by drug provings, and the *whole* of a group of symptoms of an *accidentally* occurring disease which is to be cured.

It is clear from the foregoing that Hahnemann obtained his propositions partly by induction, partly by abstraction.

§ 10.

His induction may be formulated as follows :

1. Diseases manifest themselves, as is known, by various groups of symptoms, for example, in intermittent fever, by symptomatic groups different from those of epilepsy, cardialgia, diarrhea, &c. &c.

2. Drug provings, on the healthy and the sick, have shown by experiment and observation, that, e. g. China produces a form of intermittent fever which is cured by China; Copper produces a kind of epilepsy agreeing in its form with that which it cures; Tin, a form of cardialgia similar to that which it cures; Rhubarb produces a diarrhea similar to that which it cures, &c. &c.

3. All diseases are cured by those substances which are capable of producing diseases similar to them in form.

I remark here that, for brevity's sake I only give the names of disease in common use, and not all the other characteristic symptoms which usually distinguish every disease-form mentioned in No. 2; for, it is only by the co-existence of all symptoms, that the specific entire form of any one is clearly recognizable. Here it was only necessary to set forth the form of the inductive conclusion.

This induction is no *empirical* induction, i. e., it has not arisen from the collection of similar cases, which lead the untutored masses; which, for example, from the number of deaths in any disease, reason about the cause, without knowing it; but a *rational* one, such a one as would lead to the cause from *various* cases, as here in Nos. 2 and 3. However large the *number* of cases may be, in the formation of a rational induction, it is a matter of indifference, because it is not the frequent *repetition* of the same phenomena, but the *nature of various cases*, which contain the indication for the conditions and causes under which they are possible.

So far Hahnemann's induction.

General Physiology.

§ 11.

We now continue our investigations relative to the *simile*, upon the basis of the laws of nature, in order to bring into experimental physiology, a system which can be used in therapeutics, and, by further inductions and abstractions, to connect with these natural laws the facts which arise according to the *simile*, and to explain them from these laws.

Many learned men, even, do not know what we are to understand by abstraction. *Abstraction* is. the same conclusion from the particular to the general as *Induction;* but induction shows the validity of a law *from many cases*, while abstraction shows the same validity from *one single* case and permits us to perceive what laws are already· *presupposed* in any definite assertion. Only once, for example, do I need to be told that no body can be put in motion without an "external" cause of motion; that, otherwise, it would remain in just the same state in which it is found, in order to abstract from this case, according to the law of vis inertiæ, that the occurrence of similar events is to be presupposed of the whole material world.

Hence a *law* is the form by which the constant course of phenomena from *given elements* is expressed.

To these laws, or necessary truths of mathematical abstract philosophy, belong hence: a. the law of causality; b. that of the proportion of force and velocity, or, more generally, of the proportion of effect and cause; c. the law of vis inertiæ; d. the law of the constancy of substances and forces; e. that of the equipoise of effect and countereffect, or, in brief, of reciprocal action; f. the fundamental maxim of the relationship of all motion; g. the law of the attraction of unlikes, and repulsion of likes, in contact, or at a distance.

§ 12.

That conformity to law, now, which Hahnemann had to pre-suppose, by abstraction, or which had to exist at any rate before he could form his induction, is manifold.

It lies first, as already observed in the *causal law*, but afterward also in the law of the reciprocal action of substance and forces within the organism. The first always contains a *succession* of events; the latter expresses the reciprocity of the action of substances upon each other in a definite unit, so far as the simultaneous co-existence occurs objectively. By this law the connection of the parts, as it depends upon the form of the unit, is determined and this connection of the parts again includes a dependence of the parts upon each other and upon the form of the unit.

As, for example, the law of gravitation, is a law of those dependences in the reciprocal action of our planetary system, so among others, is that of diosmosis, as we shall see, one of those dependences in the reciprocal action of our organism.

§ 13.

The third law, without which the *simile* would be inconceivable, is the law of the human form or figure, *i.e.* that of *specification*, which declares that, from an entirely equal composition of an organic body and its parts, the same form and function always arise.

This law generally considered, is self-evident from the present standpoint of natural sciences, because, for example, from the seed of an oak, a beech tree never can grow.

But this law, in its special application, determines the form for the restitution of changed, diseased parts, and, as an example thereof, I present one from physiology, and with all the more pleasure as physiological medicine places the greatest confidence in physiological prototypes.

According to the investigation of Dr. *Friedleben*, in Frankfort, (Vienna, 1860), the growth of bones in early childhood is based upon a constant destruction of constituent, and a constant formation of new, elements. The new deposits, in ever increasing proportion, take the places of the absorbed organic constituents, whence it becomes possible for the bones to change in form and size. The growth upon the outer side of the cranium, proceeding from the periosteum, occurs *independently* of that upon the inner side, which proceeds from the *Dura mater*. Hence it is not the original bone which grows after birth, on the contrary, the old crooked parietal bone must be destroyed during growth and give away to another one more arched.

Thus the law of the specification of the organism and its parts is accomplished, in other organs also, in health as well as sickness. Every changed form always corresponds with a change in composition and every new formation follows according to the law of the human form.

§ 14.

The fourth law which must have presented itself vaguely to Hahnemann's mind is that of the *constancy of substances and forces* within the organism, without which we could not conceive of the identity of the human organism, by virtue of which every change of substances and motions maintains a steadfastness of its own.

Upon the basis of this law of the *constancy of substances and forces in general*, he could at the same time pre-suppose that the effects of drugs, each for itself, always present themselves in definite parts of the organism, hence are specific, *i.e.* such as invariably return in every newly given similar case, with the necessity of natural law. Without that, the prognosis regarding the result of an administered drug, according to the law of the recollection of similar cases, would be impossible.

§ 15.

The fifth law Hahnemann very likely abstracted from daily experience ; it is the *law of life* itself, since that is living which carries the cause of its activity in itself ; in contradistinction from the activity of a machine, which is also a unit of reciprocal but mediate action, *i.e.* a force communicated by an external cause from member to member, according to the law of causation.

§ 16.

The law which finally presents these material conditions for this organic self-activity is that of the *attraction* of unlikes and the *repulsion* of likes between substances and forces in the organism.

The efficiency of every substance is confined to the limits of the space which it occupies in the organism. Hence, each substance can only act as an attractive or repulsive one to another in the proportion as much or little of the substance is present within this space. Since every substance can fill a space only by its motions, this law contains the general causes of the organic exchange of matter, which is limited by the law of *diosmosis*, and restrains a mere chemical action. It is especially the resistance of the membranes of the organism, the specific anatomical construction and molecular motion of which, produce that modification of chemical action. The diosmosis of the organic fluids, the carrier of matter, proceeds all the more rapidly and powerfully, the more unequal, on both sides of a membrane, are the fluids in motion, as regards their rapidity and chemical constitution and *the less* conceentrated they are. In this way solutions are diffused, the very solvents of which, by themselves, are not *at all miscible*. By these laws, the substances and forces of the organism find their localization at specific determined anatomical points, whence arises the possibility of the undisturbed exercise of the functions dependent thereupon.

§ 17.

The properties of substances, by virtue of which they become the causes of other changes or metamorphoses, are called their *forces*; and, if the counter-actions of substances by their forces depend upon one specific law of *immediate* reciprocal action, e. g. upon that of our organism, we call the natural phenomena therefrom arising, *processes of nature.*

Hence those substances are not equally distributed in the organism; every organ is made up of different chemical compounds, and every function begets different products or educts.

§ 18.

From this it follows again that the organism also has its *hylotopic laws*. In accordance therewith, we find Magnesia, for instance, in the teeth and in the semen ; Silicea in the blood, the bile, the urine, the bonés; fluoric acid in the bones and in the enamel of the teeth; syntonin in the muscular fibre; globuline in the blood and the crystalline lens; gluten in the bones; connective tissue in the cornea, in the cartilages; phosphoric acid in the brain; united to alkalies, in all the fluids of our organism; common salt in all fluids, and, in quantities relatively large, in the vitreous body of the eye; iron almost everywhere, but chiefly in the muscular tissue, in the globulin of the blood, but not in the globulin of the crystalline lens; lime in all the constituents of the organism, chiefly in the bones; potash, especially in the blood corpuscles and in the fluid of the flesh; the serum of the blood is rich in the salts of soda; the oxygen, hydrogen, carbonic acid and nitrogen of the atmosphere, on the other hand, are *everywhere* present in all parts of the organism, partly free, partly in composition, yet not equally diffused *in the same degree.*

§ 19.

On the other hand, we know, that the organism of man, which is thus composed of corporeal parts, similar to the elements of food, by further metamorphoses of these substances, constantly produces entirely new combinations, but only at special localities, for example, Kreatine in the red portion of the muscular flesh, and in the smooth muscles of the womb ; inosite in the flesh of the heart; pulmonic acid in the lungs, &c.   This constitutes the material contents of the organism according to the laws of its organic transposition.

§ 20.

Moreover, all the organs and their parts, are not only dependent upon definite substances, specifically belonging to them ; they not only produce entirely new combinations, specifically proceeding from them, but all this occurs and takes place, only in determinate *proportions*, which merely oscillate between a slight minimum or maximum.   Thus, for example, the pancreas contains 0.1661 per cent. of Xanthine, 0.01223 per cent. of Guanine; 1.77 per cent. of Leucine ; the muscles 0.04 per cent. of talcose earth; 0.02 per cent. of lime; 0.07 per cent. of soda, &c.

Thus the organism, throughout, is also constructed according to a Hylometric law.

§ 21.

This leads us to another law of physiological life—to that of proportional oscillation,* which informs us that the nutrition and function of the organism perpetually *oscillate* between a plus and minus, within a limit measurable by the foregoing laws.   With this law stands necessarily connected that of the periodical return of organic activities, or of *reproduction*.

The first contradicts the conclusions based upon sensation concerning the normality or abnormality of organic forms and movements, or an average calculation according to which one seeks to reduce the various forms and motions to a summary, mean relation ; it contains the mathematical law of proportionality, which rests upon the concordance of relations in which the parts of the organism in their form, function and nutrition stood, on the one side, to each other, and, on the other, to the whole.   In fact, we find, in the forms of human individuals, either a minus or a plus with regard to the never attainable ideal of æsthetics.

With this incessant change of equipoise of nutrition and function, owing to the accommodation of extremes, within definite limits, the abstract idea of health becomes a negative one, determinable at no moment of time.   The idea of health declares that a definite reality

---

* See Grungedsetze der Physiologie, Pathologie und homœopathischen Therapie.

belongs to the organism, limited, however, by the change of forms and functions.

I have mentioned here the partial law of reproduction under the name by which it is commonly known in medicine, because it is the only one which is current with the school, though it fills only one of the two schemes of the law of proportional oscillation, to wit : the momenta of the self-preservation of the organism. By reproduction, the school understands merely the restoration of that which has been expended. However, the periodical return of all organic activities, which occurs in definite proportions, also, according to *time*, should generally be understood thereby. For although, for example, according to Friedleben, many points of the skull were perfectly ossified after birth, they, subsequently, became flexible, and that, no matter what kind of food may have been given; and this change of absorption and growth frequently repeats itself, at particular months, under contemporaneous, i.e. corresponding dilatation of the fontanelles, and, in other months, again, under contraction of the same. This can take place only according to a definite law.

That *Friedleben* did not observe these functions to proceed according to the same mathematical laws, which I have, for example, demonstrated for the crisis even, in the momentum of excretion, (see Grundgesetze der Physiologie, &c.) arises from the method of his experiments. The combinatory method of naturo-philosophical investigation, which *Friedleben* adopted, is not the inductive. Its maxims contain no data of explanation, but only analytical data of comparison for the substantiation of the existence of facts, but no basis referable to laws. Hence, we are not permitted, by any means, to leave unconsidered, in this combinatory method, any momentum of time, since thus it would lose a most important part of its combination.

Friedleben paid too little regard to this, for he discontinued his experiments, on one and the same object, for days, weeks and months, because he was ignorant of that law of oscillation, and, hence, could pay it no attention.

§ 22.

Of all these laws of physiological nutrition and function, or, in one word of Nutrition, the physiological school, or so-called allopathy, with the exception of that of reproduction, knows—nothing. It can claim, however, the merit of having discovered, as far as their technical instruments reach, the most of the above-mentioned substances of which the organism is composed. Yet it does not understand how to show, from all these empiric acquisitions, to what purpose all its own discoveries might be used in Therapeutics, since no fact judges, and empiricism enumerates only facts. Hence, the pseudo-therapeutics of the physiological school is compelled to proceed merely according to authority and tradition, and can by no means be proven to rest upon logic, and, still less, upon natural laws.

General Pathology.

§ 23.

The law of vis inertiæ informs us that *all changes* of the body have an external cause, because no body, by its own power, can change its own state into another, but can only change the state of another body.

Herein the fundamental law of *pathological* nutrition and function is expressed.

The idea of this change, thus, rests upon the permanent presence, upon the constancy, the persistence of the forms of the organism, side by side with the change of its conditions, its accidents, properties and relations.

If, accordingly, even the conception of health exists only in the idea, so, on the contrary, no idea of disease can be formed, since only its realities exist, which the reason cannot excogitate and the imagination cannot create; for we know of material *causes* of disease, which operate constantly, so long as the conditions for them are present in the organism.

§ 24.

A change observed, then, in the whole or a part of the organism, must, hence, always point to a material *external* cause, even though it be unknown, no matter whether it were inherited from parents, or accidentally, or intentionally received into, or developed in our organism, by a course of life opposed to the laws of nature. The substances of the organism do not arise or disappear in it, they merely *change* their conditions, no matter how often they are renewed or removed. As soon, however, as an external cause has changed the condition of all the substances and forces of the organism, it dies at once, i.e., its self-activity is lost.

That happens, however, only from fatal quantities of qualities, and the action of a substance, not pertaining to the ends of its existence, arises, as a rule, from smaller quantities; hence, confines itself to a limited sphere of action, determined by the laws of the attraction of dissimilars and the repulsion of similars, consequently to a *specific* sphere of action. Yet, it is clear that, with the transformation of an atom of cartilage, for instance, an atom of salt is, also, decomposed, which had formed a unit with the former, &c.

Therefrom result, in distinction from the physiological, *pathological* hylotopic and metabolic phenomena, &c., which naturally are of far less compass.

§ 25.

An example from Virchow's latest work, his Cellular Pathology, p. 193, on gout, may illustrate this :

"If we examine the articular tophus of an arthritic patient, we find it composed of very fine needle-like crystalline secretions, of all possible sizes, consisting of urate of soda, amongst which, at most, here and there, a pus or blood-corpuscle appears. Here, then, we have to do with a corporeal substance, which, as a rule, is excreted by the kidneys, and, indeed, so copiously that, even within the kidneys, deposits thereof are formed, and especially in the urinary canaliculi of the medullary substance, large crystals of urate of soda are collected, sometimes to the extent of plugging up the canaliculus, If, however, this secretion does not proceed regularly, then an accumulation of urates subsequently takes place in the blood, as is demonstrated by a very convenient method of *Garrod*. Then, at last, deposits begin at other points, not through the whole body, not equally in all parts, but at particular points and according to certain rules."

§ 26.

In this example, we find a confirmation of the premises based upon the natural law laid down in the preceding paragraph, connected, however, with other conclusions, which show that, to Prof. Virchow, the laws of nature governing such processes are wholly unknown. For all this occurs, not according to certain, i.e., indeterminate laws, but according to the laws which have been already mentioned, for, by virtue of the permanent identity of the organism, *the same laws* prevail, in general, as well in its pathological as in its physiological states, since everything which changes, or can be changed in the organism, belongs but to the kind of changes according to which it, i.e., the organism, exists itself. Were not this the case, a cure would, *a priori*, be Inconceivable. The rules, or laws, according to which these processes take place, Virchow passes in silence, and also leaves unanswered a question not to be evaded, why those deposits begin at particular points, &c.

§ 27.

According to the laws of nature, just set forth, a group of symptoms, to which the name of gout is given, can only exist *generally*, never *specially;* as little as there exists a special scarlatina, or any other inflammation, &c.; for there are, always, only specific material causes of disease, and, in addition thereto, the material conditions of the individual organism. The latter, within the changeable in the organism, are so very variable, that the school has already labored to construct the most manifold *individual* differences.

We witness, for example, in small-pox, an exquisite localization of the morbid cause upon the surface of the skin; but, for the rest, there is, in every *individual,* a different course of the process, according to the quantity, quality and relation of the substances and forces of the organism. Hence, in every individual, though the cause is the same, a different group of symptoms must appear, accompanying the exanthem.

More manifold groups of symptoms are produced, for instance, by the marsh miasm; with one, the usual form of intermittent fever with the previous chill, the subsequent heat and the concluding sweat, appears on particular days, at particular hours; with another, violent facial neuralgia: with a third, jaundice, even, both without the accompaniment of that usual fever form; with a fourth, we have chill, bloody expectoration during the fever and then sweat. But, to all these varied pathological forms, from the same cause, the general symptom of periodicity adheres, and, when this is cured, almost always, complete health returns, as if nothing had happened.

§ 28.

Without detailing any more forms of disease, it is clear, from these few, that the *co-existence* of these phenomena, with the other individual activities of the organism, always presents a *specifically* changed, consequently, a pathological form of the whole of its reciprocal action, so that each one of them must be considered as a peculiar *species,* as here, for example, many species belong to the genus, intermittent fever.

From these investigations, we see clearly the difference, so important for a scientific therapeutics, between the cause of disease and the conditions with regard to its sphere of activity in the individual organism. The *effect* is the consequence, owing to the existence of a *cause.* The condition is the result of the specific composition, dependent upon the substances and forces of the organism, which is different with every individual. The cause is thus a single object, the condition is the co-existence of organic activities. For these reasons, the same morbific cause may meet various conditions of counter-action, and, just like the marsh miasm, beget various forms of disease, i.e., groups of symptoms, every part of which deserves consideration as well as the rest. Therefore, on account of the co-existence of the whole with its parts, the whole of the changed form of the reciprocal action of the organism is to be kept in view, in all cases, as regards the co-existence of the whole with its parts; hence, is to be taken as an *object existing by itself*. Consequently, in Homœopathy, no regard is paid to one or the other symptom by itself, to single peculiarities or predicates and characteristics of the genus of a disease, which, by themselves considered, would always be unintelligible, and lead only, as in Allopathy or physiological medicine, to injurious curative efforts.

§ 29·

From these individualities, the physiological school, on the basis of some prominent peculiarity, has constructed various so-called bodily constitutions. It speaks, for example, of a feeble constitution. This is, clearly, an indefinite idea, of no advantage in practice. The conditions of such a bodily constitution consist in this, that it (the constitution) has less resistance to oppose to external influences than the so-called *robust*. But, from the laws of diosmosis, we learn that it is the membranes whose construction should furnish that resistance, and, therefrom, moreover, the material quantities and qualities ensue, which must be regulated by art. In the so-called *phlegmatic* constitution, of the physiological school, this relation appears still more clearly, though it is unknown to the school, and, even if this relation were known, it would not know how to render aid according to the laws of nature. In this constitution, according to experience, a large percentage of water exists in the whole organization, owing to which a morbific cause is again confronted by a sphere of action quite different from that, to offer another example of the so-called *constitutio pasta*, which manifests itself by a greater per centage of carbon; each one of these various qualities will, none the less, have in readiness, and be able to produce, counter-actions different from the others.

Hence, look at it from what direction we may, there exist for therapeutics none but pathological summary forms of organization, but never single symptoms.

§ 30.

If these varieties, if such so-called bodily constitutions, can only be set down among *pathological* qualities, there exist, moreover, also, *permanent morbific causes*, so long as the conditions for their diffusion in the organism are not cured.

While the law of specification presents to us the inner and outer form and composition of the organism, it furnishes us, at the same time, the indication for the differences arising from these permanent causes, the *chemical changes* or *substitutions* which the organism has to suffer, in its substances of nutrition and function, not for a moment only, but, sometimes, even, for the whole life.

The organism requires, it is true, definite substances for its structure, as well as a specific chemical composition of its organs, tissues and fluids, for each of its functions; but, we know, from homœopathic drug-provings, that the substances of nutrition, which are used to meet the supply of wasted tissues, or for the formation of new, cannot substitute each other, although many substances of nutrition have, at the same time, to substitute various function-substances which may be especially observed in chronic diseases, as, for example, sulphur substitutes oxygen.

As in nutrition, so, also, in Therapeutics, we have to keep one eye fixed, not merely on affinities, as Virchow would have us, but, also, upon the *substitutions*, as they are called in chemistry, of the substances of definite anatomical localities by others, thus, not merely upon physiological and pathological hylotopic and metabolic processes, but, also, upon physiological and pathological hyloteretic processes. Hydrogen, for instance, can be substituted, not only in dead organic bodies, but, also, in the organism, by Chlorine, Bromine, Iodine, Fluorine, Nitrous Acid, and, in the same manner, can Sulphur, Selenium and Tellurium supply the place of the oxygen of the organism, while the latter substances, again, act as substitutes for each other. Upon these relations the Homœopathic doctrine of antidotes is based, according to the law of reciprocal action, as well as the doctrine of the conditional succession of remedies, to be found only in Homœopathy.

For instance, in many cases of intermittent, neither Digitalis nor Selenium nor Kreosote can be given after Quinine, else the fever will return.

Have such distinctions ever been heard of in the Physiological school?

§ 31.

The confirmation of such hyloteretic phenomena may daily be observed in Homœopathic practice, and most plainly in all forms of disease pointing to a constitution chiefly characterized by an excess of water, or to another, manifesting itself by the impeded reception of Ozone.

But it is worthy of remark that the forms of disease in the first bodily constitution have the character of *Hahnemann's* Sycosis, or Rademacher's constitution, curable by Natrum Nitricum; while those in the latter constitution correspond to the character of Hahnemann's Psora, or with that constitution of Rademacher, for which copper and sulphur serve as remedies.

This concurrence explains itself from the *chemical* relations of the remedies indicated and approved by the law of similarity, in the sycotic and psoric forms, since the former, viz., Natr. Sulph., Natr. mur., Acid nitr., Iodine, Bromine, &c., diminish the action of hydrogen upon the blood and tissues; the latter, e. g., copper, sulphur, phosphorus, camphor, &c., increase the action of oxygen, i.e., ozone, upon the same structures.

§ 32.

Hahnemann incurred much more blame, from his opponents, on account of his Psora, than did *Virchow*, on account of his Leucæmia, which sprang from the same process of reasoning. *Hahnemann* observed that many diseases have the character in common of being similar to those which were frequently observed, in his time, after suppressed itch. *Virchow* found that many diseases have this in common, that they are attended with an excess of white blood. *Hahneman* arranged those diseases under the head of Psora; Virchow, likewise, made a genus of his Leucæmia, although he, at the same time, acknowledged that it arose from *previously* diseased organs, or their parts. Now, which inference is the better? Yet, Virchow received unlimited applause. Both inferences, however, are based only upon the category of Quality, and are of an equally subjective character, and, hence, liable to important corrections; they do not suffice, however, to invalidate the facts from which they are deduced, as the physiological school has done with Psora. Yet, a school ought to know that a mistake in a conclusion allows of correction, and that the truth should not be rejected with the error, and, that, in absence of proof, facts should not be rejected without further investigation. In no case is the conclusion the object of itself; on the contrary, it remains only a supposition, so long as it is not referred to laws.

We know, however, that the school does not like to consider matters which have not originated with it. In such a case, it always has the fig leaf of *negation* at hand, for its ignorance. This fig leaf, however, is a thread-bare cloak, for a negation is no opinion; it assumes the right of refraining from noticing the matter. The difference between Hahnemann and Virchow merely consists in this, that, in Hahnemann's time, the science of mathematical abstract philosophy was quite crude, which was no longer the case in Virchow's time.

§ 33.

To return, once more, to the permanent causes of the diseases of the bodily constitutions, &c., which Hahnemann discovered, I quote again, first from Virchow's Cellular Pathology, p. 196, where he had just spoken of Gout, the Salts of Silver and pyæmia, and continues thus :—

" Since we have learned to recognize, not only bodily parts, but, also, certain chemical substances, as the factors of dyscrasiæ, which have a duration, longer or shorter, according as the supply of these parts and substances continues, a longer or a shorter time, we may briefly return to the question whether, side by side of these forms, a kind of dyscrasia is demonstrable, *in consequence of which the blood appears as the permanent. carrier of definite changes. These questions we must answer in the negative.* The more manifest a clearly demonstrable impurification of the blood with certain substances is, the more evident is the relatively acute course of the process. It is most likely that just the very forms regarding which, in view of the insufficiency of the therapeutie results, we most fondly console (? !) ourselves with the idea of having to do with a deeply seated and incurable chronic dyscrasia, depend, in the least, upon original change of the blood; in the majority of these very cases, we have to do with extensive changes of certain organs or single parts. I can not maintain that we have reached the end of the investigation ; I can only say that every means of microscopic or chemical analysis has hitherto been used without avail; as regards the hematological knowledge of this process; that, on the other hand, in most cases we can demonstrate essential changes of larger or smaller complexes of organic parts, and that, in general, the probability increases everyday, that, even *here,* we shall recognize the dyscrasia as a secondary phenomenon, dependent upon certain organie points."

§ 34.

But, what, if I may ask, what had made those organs or separate parts, those organic points, sick? What can chemistry decide if it, itself, furnishes combinations of organic substances, the separate parts of which it subsequently can not recognize again by its re-agents, as, for example, the combination of chlorine with organic bodies, by which not even the chemical type of those bodies is changed? And what can microscopy decide, which is as little able as chemistry to discover what material changes the milk of an angry woman has undergone which throws the nursing child into fatal convulsions?

And if chemistry and microscopy can not be the final arbiters in such inquiries, and for this end are utterly impotent, whence does the physiological school obtain its remedies for diseases? It either treats "by ear," (auscultation and percussion,) or comforts itself with assumed incurability, instead of taking hold of the logical instruments in cases where the technical have proved insufficient.

If the origin of a so-called dyscratic impurification of the blood could be explained merely by an extensive change of certain organs, or parts of organs, and the blood could not be considered as the permanent agent of definite changes in other parts, the element in which we live, and which stands in immediate and permanent relation with the blood, the atmosphere, would then contain, in its constituents, unchangeable elements, which, as we know, is not the case, as we may learn, for example, by the excretion of carbon in expiration. In consequence of the electricity of the air, for instance, the respiratory motions are not only reduced, but the quantity of excreted carbonic acid is diminished; while transpiration, evacuation of urine and thirst are increased. Such changes, in the substances and forces of the atmosphere, are the known causes of the most various diseases, acute as well as chronic. In this instance, it is not necessary to refer to cholera, its precursors and sequelæ; but it suffices, for example, to allude to the chronic changes of the blood owing to marsh miasm.

Many men who live near standing water are exempt from intermittent fever for months, and it frequently attacks them, with violence, not before the summer of the year following, although they have spent half a year in a very dry region and show no perceptible change in the liver and spleen.

§ 35.

Should we not indulge the expectation that the teachers of universities, in case of diseased organs, or their parts, would think of something better than to declare them to be agents of the so-called

Dyscrasiæ, and that they would remember that nothing can originate by itself, but must have an external cause? Under such circumstances, it may agree very well, in their teaching, with the more easy art of experiment and operations of all kinds, but very badly with the art, far more difficult to acquire, of observation by means of logical instruments.

The blood, as we well know, appears to be the agent of permanent causes of consecutive changes, a fact, I admit, which may have remained unknown to the school, but not to the practicing physician. Its quality is always the product of a combination of the substances of the atmosphere with those peculiar to the organism, and the atmosphere is able to change the quality of the blood, and, with it, the whole organism, so entirely, that the pathological constitutions known to the oldest physicians, find, in the atmosphere, one of the fundamental conditions of their existence.

§ 36.

While the structure of the blood-corpuscles furnishes the independent regulator for the reception of atmospheric substances, it is, however, sometimes so relaxed that this function becomes insufficient, a condition which, as a necessary consequence, must produce a permanent reaction upon the whole organism.

As an example of this I select *Chlorosis*, since it is one of the most common diseases, yet, from year to year, a most sad *crux medicorum* of physiological medicine; in men, the school calls the thing anæmia.

Homœopathy knows from its drug provings, that there is a kind of Chlorosis accompanied by symptoms, which agree perfectly, in form, with the symptoms produced in proving Glauber's Salts, while many other forms agree with the symptoms of the provings of Sulphur, Nitric acid, Iodine, &c. Now, Glauber's Salts, when absorbed, acts within the organism, as it does without, in a manner by which it reduces the action of hydrogen upon the blood-corpuscles to a very low degree; Nitric acid and Iodine act as substitution remedies of the Hydrogen in the blood. If we have a case of chlorosis before us, that corresponds with the pathogenetic symptoms of Sulphur, there is either a want of Sulphur in the albumen of the blood, or the action of oxygen upon the blood is diminished. In the former case, the Sulphur acts as a nutrition-remedy; in the latter, as a function-remedy, i.e., it acts, in this case, as a substitution-remedy for the oxygen. Therefore, by the way, any other distinction of remedies, than that between nutrition and function remedies, can not be made, because these two motions, form the two chief factors in the exchange of matter.

Hence,for experts, the Homœopathic drug provings, not only answer for indications, according to the law of similarity, *a priori*, but also *a posteriori*. From the *chemical* reaction of their substances upon organic structures, they admit of inferences as to the corresponding bodily constitution, as we have just now seen. Both conclusions form mutual complements in such a way that one may lead to the other. Therefore, the knowledge of the bodily constitutions indicated by *Hahnemann* in his Chronic Diseases and, afterwards, more fully elaborated, often leads more promptly to a choice between two or more remedies apparently indicated, by the law of similarity, than the recalling, which is often wearisome, of all the characteristic symptoms of the same. Furthermore, as far as this selection is a proper one, it always agrees with the law of similarity.

Whoever, then, wishes in the shortest way, to gain an insight into the various bodily constitutions, must, for this reason, study the Homœopathic drug-provings of the substances belonging thereto, Glauber's Salts, Sulphur, Iron, &c., &c.

§ 37.

Within the compass of this manifold mutual activity of substances and forces, within this relation between morbific cause and the organism, a state of immunity of definite parts against the morbific cause manifests itself, to the act of diagnosis, just as plainly as does the proportionate change in other parts; the first according to the law of the repulsion of likes, the latter according to the law of attraction of unlikes, as experience confirms, at the sick bed, every day.

General Therapeutics.

§ 38.

Finally, by these pathological laws the question is answered, what is to be cured? What is to be the object of therapeutics? In answer to the former it is certainly *not the parts which have remained healthy*, as such, for they have shown that they enjoy immunity against the morbific cause; they must, however, be considered the agents which carry the remedies to the diseased parts, which, already affected with deranged nutrition and function,naturally enough can not be restored, by themselves, to their former condition, but only by art, provided such restoration can not be accomplished simply by the nature and mediation of the parts remaining healthy, i.e., according to the above mentioned laws of nutrition. 'If this, however, were possible in a case of disease, it would be no *cure by art*, but a spontaneous *recovery*, since, in nature, every thing occurs without human assistance, and *art* is that which man, in full purpose, strives to accomplish.

From these propositions it follows that the *curability* or *incurability* of any disease does not depend, solely, upon its intensity, but chiefly upon the quality, quantity, and relation of the parts remaining healthy.

§ 39.

It is inconceivable, according to the previously detailed laws of nutrition and function, which ever remain the same, for physiological as well as pathological states, that a cure could ever be brought about in any other way than by one similar to the disease ; it is accordingly just as inconceivable that any one should undertake to accomplish a cure by any other agent than such as we *knew beforehand* not only acted under the same *conditions*, but also upon the same anatomical localities and physiological functions over which the morbific cause had control. On the other hand, it must stand in an *inverse* relation of attraction and repulsion to the substances and forces *changed* by the morbific cause, that is to say, the drug, although describing the same orbit of action as the materies morbi, must bear a relation of opposition to the nutritive and functional movements changed by the morbific cause.

§ 40.

According to these demands conformable to natural law, nature itself, in fact, offers us the organic conditions for the execution of such cures ; for no part and no cell of the organism consists of but *one substance,*and none of these parts can, by any morbific cause whatever, be separated or isolated from its surroundings. Hence, if, for example, a cell membrane becomes sick, it can be cured through the medium of its outer *surroundings;* if it is the intercellular fluid it may find its cure through the membrane ; if it is the cell nucleus it may find its cure through the intercellular fluid—a scheme which answers for all cases.

Although the specific anatomical construction of the partition walls, for example, of the blood cells, is decisive both in an inward and outward direction, with reference to the diffusion of various chemical and graduated fluids, the gaseous as well as the liquid, yet the whole function depends mainly upon the *supply from the surroundings,* on which account, also, the contents of the blood cells in

water, fat, albumen, globuline, hæmatine, chlorine, iron, alkalies,
phosphoric acid, are always found *oscillating* within certain limits.

§ 41.

A change, a minus or plus, of any one of these substances, beyond
these limits, announces itself, by reason of the dependence of the
whole upon the parts, by its results upon the entire organism,
by its symptoms, much more plainly than it would be possible by
chemical or microscopical analysis of the blood. There are, for instance, chlorotic girls and women whose blood, at first, suffers no
lack of red corpuscles, but contains an excess of water, which
if not by technical means, can yet be proven by the diagnosis of
the group of symptoms. One species of this genus chlorosis never
is accompanied with leanness, but with rotundity of form, and an
equally diffused pallor over the whole surface of the skin; this form
is frequently attended with vertigo; the constant irritability accompanying this condition is turned into the best humor by a fluid stool.
These patients are short-breathed, without marked palpitation of the
heart, complain of toothache and pains in the liver, &c., and every
thing is aggravated during damp weather. Or, there are mothers
whose milk suffers a lack of phosphate of lime, which chemical analysis can not tell us, while the skull bones of the children indicate
this lack, since they have permanently ceased to grow.

Thus *nature indicates to us the way to a cure with the clearest tokens;*
thus the outer groups of symptoms give us to know the inner condition of the body with that exactness which results from the *whole* of
an organic pathological reciprocal activity, and leads us to *essential,*
i.e. homœopathic indications, of the necessity of which allopathy
speaks only in dreams.

§ 42.

The object for an essential indication, to be supplied or removed
by means of a cure, hence, can not be a single function or several, as
the physiological school thinks, but, simply and solely, separate substances and their forces.

Now another question arises: How can we obtain the knowledge
of such substances and forces, which can effect such a restoration of
that which has been lost by the morbific cause, or such a removal of
the surplus which it has produced, and make full restitution of the
changes produced according to relation, quantity and quality?

It may well be assumed, that what has been said is quite sufficien to lead to the conviction, that this question is even now superfluous; it is however a necessary question, on account of the ignorance of the opposition, on account of the notorious ignorance of the opponents of Homœopathy, of all the laws of nature and the events which flow therefrom.

§ 43.

Virchow thinks that, if biology and ætiology shall once become complete, then we, i.e. Allopathy, will at last have a rational therapeia. Consenting to the truthful confession that physiological medicine, as yet, *has no rational therapeia*, we must only fear, that, even if biology and ætiology were complete, it would not, even then, have attained to any rational therapeutics; for these studies do not lead us to the knowledge of the properties of a remedy, which can be obtained, neither from one nor the other, of these realms of science; otherwise, in order to change the direction of the bed of a river, we should have to ask its source, and the formation of its bed, for advice.

§ 44.

Hahnemann proceeded, without much ado, as do the causes of disease. He took, as they do, the entire organism in its so-called physiological state, and introduced, into the most unlike individuals, the same substances as morbific causes, in order to see what the result would be.

This inventive maxim was all the more admirable, since the laws of nutrition were utterly unknown to him.

He presupposed, also, as has been said, upon the ground of his experiments, the prevalence of natural laws, and could therefore calculate upon the discovery of *new laws of nature*, i.e., *upon the constant, though new, course of events from the elements newly presented by him;* upon the production of the most varied *new* pathological hylotopic, hyloteretic, and metabolic, &c.. phenomena in the organism, in consequence of his drug provings.

That proves, at the same time, that he knew his task to be threefold, for he experimented precisely according to *the laws of the art of experiment*, which, as their works testify, do not seem to be known to all of the natural philosophers of the present day.

In order to learn the nature of such substances, in their connection with the organism, he solved *one* problem of this art, by changing the individualities in which action and counter-action of one and the same substance must present themselves, according to his experiment; the second, by connecting therewith, the change of time, of place, and of circumstances; and the *third*, by attempting to measure the quantities of substances thereby used.

He proceeded, as can be shown, according to these rules, and his followers took the example of the great master as a guide, in order to extend the new science.

§ 45.

They found it confirmed, that the diseases artificially produced by Hahnemann and themselves in this manner, were, as to their diagnosticable forms, and their group of symptoms, strikingly concordant and hence, similar to many of those originating from accidental causes : that, thus, many of those substances which they proved upon the healthy, described the same orbit of action, within the organism, as many, and indeed, most of the morbific causes. These forms of mutual similarities, *from different causes*, increased in the same measure as they experimented, with different substances of the outer world, according to these rules.

We can not proceed any further in our investigation till we have shown by an example, to those not familiar with these matters, these subjects invested in the usual garb of their own way of thinking.

§ 46.

I select again, for this purpose, an example from Virchow, from the page preceding the previous quotation, about gout. "We know, that, when any one uses the salts of silver, they penetrate the tissues : if we do not administer them in their characteristic corrosive, destructive form, the silver enters into a combination, (the nature of which is not, at present, sufficiently understood,) in the tissues, and produces, at the point of application, if it is used long enough, a change of color. A patient who received a solution of Argent. nitr. Nov. 10th in v. Græfe's, Clinic for external application, used as a conscientious patient, the remedy, up to the present time ; the result thereof was that his conjunctiva had assumed an intensely brown, almost black, appearance. The examination of a portion removed, showed that the elementary tissues had taken up a part of the silver, in such a manner as to produce a light yellow brown color on the entire surface of the conjunctiva, while the deposit had taken place, more deeply, only in the fine elastic fibers of the conjunctiva and the intermediate parts; the true basic substances, were perfectly free from it. Quite similar deposits, however happened also, in remote organs. Our collection contains the very rare preparation of the kidneys of a man who had taken Arg. nitr. a long time internally for epilepsy. In the Malpighian corpuscles of the kidneys, where the peculiar secretion occurred, a blackish-blue discoloration of the whole vascular membrane took place, which was confined to this portion, of the cortical substance, appearing again in a similar, though less distinct, manner, in the intermediary substance of the medullary canaliculi. Hence, in the whole kidney, then, except those parts which represent the special points of secretion, only those parts were changed which correspond to the last capillary subdivision in the medullary substance."

Besides that, Virchow remarks, p. 199, ' Just as the salt of silver is not deposited in the lung, but passes right through it, to be deposited in the kidneys, or skin, so an ichorous fluid, from a cancerous tumor-may pass through the lungs without changing them, while it may how, ever awake malignant changes in a point far remote, for instance, in the bone of a distant part."

§ 47.

In this example we see the previously adduced laws, resulting from drug provings, confirmed in every respect. I must always furnish examples from the facts observed by our very adversaries. so that these, at least, can not be disputed away. But, in natural sciences, we have to do with the connection of facts, observed with the natural laws controlling them, if, while ever so numerous, they are not meant to be practically useless. But the physiological school knows no law With it, faith in authority always occupies the place of laws of nature, or, faith in tradition, or, the recommendation of others, as motive for the use of drugs. Hence, notwithstanding its innumerable one-sided experiments it is always betrayed into absurdities in its indications.

§ 48.

Even Virchow used that quotation about gout, as well as this abont the silver salt, only for the purpose of explaining the idea of Metastasis of the ancients. The old physicians sought to explain, with this idea, those cases of disease which arise, even to-day, according to *Virchow's* own brilliant discovery, in consequence of embolism or thrombosis. But why does *Virchow*, in judging of this matter, combine mechanical effects with processes of nature ? By this confusion of two subjects. *Virchow* was hindered from seeing, that there exists still another basis of classification, for the knowledge of which it would, of course have been necessary to search for the law of nature inductively.

That we call a subordinate standpoint, which deems itself obliged to retain antiquated ideas in place of inductive conclusions from truly precious experiments, and even to enlarge them without reason ; for it belongs to the laws of the lower train of thought to connect given effect with any previous event, according to the *habit* of our power of association. In view of those examples of gout and the silver salt,one can speak of metastasis only so long as he is ignorant of the law of specification, of attraction and repulsion in the organism, according to which laws, it (the organism) is *compelled* to bring forth its physiological as well as pathological hylotopic phenomena, so long as he can not forbear from thrusting into one and the same circle of ideas, this self–activity of the organism, with the consequences of purely mechanical action, e.g. that of thrombosis.

§ 49.

Now, it is true, even an artificially produced hylotopic process, may result from homœopathic drug provings, and since we have just been speaking of gout, one that corresponds to this form of disease.

By these drug provings, for instance, we learn that Benzoic acid produces pains in the metatarsal joint of the great toe ; that the pains which it produces, frequently and suddenly change their location— wander to the chest and produce continuous dry cough, even asthma and palpitation of the heart, accompanied by a hard accelerated pulse, fever, heat and perspiration ; that it may affect almost all the joints of the body in succession, especially also the knee-joint, even producing swelling there. It irritates of course, applied only internally, not only the conjunctiva of the eye, but produces also, in the whole bulb, a sense of pressure,and begets an exquisite angina tonsillaris, pains in the kidneys and bladder ; besides there is not always hippuric acid in the urine.

In this briefly expressed homœopathic drug proving we have a formal concordance, a *homoion pathos* with arthritis vaga, and it can scarcely be better given.

§ 50.

I shall not err, if I reckon Benzoic acid among the function-remedies, i.e. as not being one of the substances of which the organism is composed; it is only an occasional product of organic functions.

If now I ask one of these professors or clinicians, who plume themselves so very much on their knowledge, what they think of the mode action of such function-remedies, I get no answer; at least nothing

4

of the kind is contained in any of their writings, nor in their lectures, yet they teach that such remedies, not related to the organism, should be given to the sick, in quantities which exceed all natural bounds and which can by no means be justified. Nor do they tell us anywhere that the nutrition-remedies, i.e. those out of which the organism itself is composed, will operate according to the laws of growth in nutrition even if they are given singly as medicines, for this would contain a verdict against the quantities used by them, by which they torture the diseased organism without helping it.

[§ 51.

If, now, as regards even the action of function-remedies, we look about for a scientific basis, we cannot but infer that, since they do not serve restoration, they can manifest their action only in a manner reminding us of the law of chemical substitution.

But the physiological school, closely encompassed in the magic circle of its habits, requires from a remedy, as from any externally applied cause, a single i.e. a mediate, proportional action according to the law applicable to machinery, but very seldom, and, only for a moment, applicable to the organism ; it forgets, in the expectation of such events, the other counter-actions of the organism. Since its capacity of observation is confined merely to the effect of greater quantities, it never remembers that, in order to cure, it has to *restore* changed functions but not to over excite and over-stimulate them, beyond measure, a process by which a new disease is always added to the old one. It wishes absolutely to *beget* an effect, but not *to produce one conditionally.* It proceeds from the maxim, to wit: like causes, like effects; but never considers that the difference betwen Agens and Patiens is illusory.

§ 52.

Homœopathy, on the contrary, discovered, with its drug provings, and with the laws of nature, for a guide, quite a number of material relations. It knows, for instance, that Aconite produces congestion of blood in the lungs, accompanied with stitches in the side, fever, &c: that it is no nutrition-remedy for the organism, hence by *substitution* only, can produce the known changes of function which, if the proving is carried still farther, may lead also to changes of nutrition. It knows that Phosphorus, for example, can not be merely a nutrition-remedy of the blood, as it produces, according to those provings, a decrease of the volume of the blood-corpuscles and, likewise congestion in the lungs. By the treatment of pneumonias, with these remedies, Homœopathy gained the further experience that Aconite produces a cure in the first stage, and Phosphorus even in the second, and most dangerous stage of this disease. Since, now, the drug provings led to indications for the patient and, the confirmation of the homœopathic suppositions, the cure followed right afterwards; thus from the given conditions, for example, from the effect of Aconite in Pneumonia, a constant course of events is established, at the same time; consequently a curative method applied according to *natural law*. What other question could yet be asked of science ?

Such homœopathic experiments and deductive confirmations are exactly of the same value as those of chemistry, since, in both sciences, a value can only attach to that which, from given conditions, always produces the same constant course of events.

§ 53.

Even in its very cradle, Homœopathy has kept itself above false conclusions, for the formation of its indications. It draws, still to make use of the same example, a comparison between the *unity* of the group of symptoms in Arthritis vaga, and the *unity* of symptoms which Benzoic acid produces in the organism.

But, as there exists an analytical and a synthetical conclusion, there exists, also, an analytical and synthetical *comparison*. If, for instance, I compare Benzoic acid and Colchicum, in their various properties, with each other, by enumerating their special distinctive marks, I compare *analytically*. If, on the contrary, I compare Benzoic acid and Colchicum, with one another, in their reciprocal action with the interior of the organism, I get two different new units of comparison of groups of symptoms, and neither in the one, nor in the other, are the distinctive features of both of these substances found again. Hence, the comparison takes place here by the *connection* of the law of organic *reciprocal action* with both substances, hence, is *synthetic*. If, finally, I compare the unit of comparison, from the groups of symptoms of Benzoic acid, and of Arthritis vaga, by synthesis, with the law of *similarity*, then the mode of establishing the homœopathic indications is logically expressed; it is the summing up of the units of comparison under the law according to which the "curantur" of the simile takes place.

§ 54.

The physiological school has a similar synthesis for its indication in the Contraria contrariis, which means that diseases must be cured by remedies acting in a manner opposite to the former.

This synthesis, however, is connected with the causal law. This *contrarium*, by the way, originated with *Hahnemann*, who threw it at the feet of his opponents as an apple of discord. They knew then, as little as now, what thus happened to them, since, even at that time, they took possession of this apple at once, and form their indications from it, to this very day. Thus, they set up as an indication, what with *Hahnemann*, was the *result* of the immediate action and counteraction, within the organism, upon the basis of his indication, according to the simile, § 8, and thus confound, in the most extraordinary manner, the effect with the indication, hence, the result with the cause; their comparisons inevitably lead, and still must lead, to erroneous perceptions at the bed-side.

§ 55.

The physiological school makes comparisons at the sick-bed between a predicate, a token or symptom of diseases, and the general mode of action of this or that drug in large quantities; for, with this school, there is, in every disease, only *one* symptom to be combatted, and every drug has, as far as that school is concerned, only *one* action against it. If this were not the case, then this contrarium would be the most perfect nonsense.

Thus it makes, first of all, comparisons, for example, between the symptoms of a patient affected by gout, and those of a healthy man with regard to his mode of living, and finds that excess and sumptuous living, frequently occasions all that is comprised under the general head of gout; while the abstemious and poor remain, as a rule, free from it. Hence, although the cow has already been stolen, it prescribes, as a main thing, dietetic and prophylactic measures, then emetics and purgatives, for the exportation of the unprofitable stock. Since, moreover, gout frequently makes its attack after checked perspiration, it applies remedies to which it ascribes diaphoretic properties, &c. It found, however, that the over-excitement of organic functions with stimulating substances, often leaves it, not only in the lurch, but is, also, likely to be followed by injurious, though unintentional, results. Hence, in this juncture, it presently turns with affection to vapor baths, though it observed that these, even, are not without danger. From similar comparisons, it administers Colchicum, too, in the idea that it can eliminate, by this " diuretic," as they call it, what the morbific cause has produced; this, however, is impossible, since, from no effect can we conclude as to the cause. If any vascular congestion is observed in the part affected, then, by way of comparison with the laws of hydrostatics, outside of the organism, it prescribes for it an elevated position, in order to impede the return of the venous blood as little as possible, although it knows, on the other hand, that the circulation of the blood, and, especially, congestion, takes place chiefly against the law of gravitation. But if, as is natural enough, none of these means should bring relief, then it applies chloroform, as that can soothe other pains; and if, even then, no permanent improvement manifests itself, it gets vexed and takes refuge in various mixtures, Colchicum and Opium being the favorites. But if even this terminates in no good, all which it has occasioned does not yet prompt it to reflect and ask, whether any of all these proceedings can be read of in the book of Nature? It rather prefers to let things take their course, as pleases God, till the appearance of some new violent symptom impels it to array itself again in opposition against that. The necessarily occurring debility of the patient finally warns these allopathic physicians again, to quit, at last, all these hostile attacks which war against the organism and never reach the cause of the disease; and thus it goes on, *ad infinitum*, with this pitiable symptomatic method.

§ 56.

The law of nature, which is the basis of the treatment according to the indication of the *Contrarium*, is, hence, the law of causality, that of the necessary connection of cause and effect; hence, in this school, ideas such as the following are synonymous : diuretics and the expulsion of uric acid from the gouty nodosities; constipation and purgatives; suppressed perspiration and diaphoretics, &c.; ideas which require but little reasoning, hence, are mere comparisons of properties among themselves, lacking every organic comparative merit, which should be able to supply the place of the subject or object in the conclusion. Every conclusion must be formed from, at least, two ideas, one of which has the form of the object, the other the form of the predicate, and every indication, even if it has arisen from comparison, must exhibit the form of a conclusion. Since, however, the physiolog‐ical school can only draw analytical comparisons, between single *predicates*, none of its indications can, for this reason, be called a proper conclusion. It could, at most, claim the *contràrium* of its indication as an objective idea, only, however, to fare, in its conclusion, worse than before.

§ 57.

What, now, is there in the indication of Colchicum for gout, so
fondled by that school? It is worth the little trouble to answer this
question, for, notwithstanding its confession that this indication often
punishes that school with lack of success, yet it cannot altogether
desist from its use, since, in some cases diagnosticated as gout, it
afforded relief contrary to all expectations.

According to the homœopathic drug provings, Colchicum produces
chilliness and shivering, even in a warm temperature. Heat, generally,
does not set in till night, and, in the morning a sour-smelling sweat
breaks out. The pulse varies in frequency and, often, is irregular.
Furthermore, it produces boring headache, especially over the eyes;
inflammation of the eyes, dimness of sight, weeping and white spots
on the cornea, pains in the ears, inflammation of the nasal mucous
membrane, and of the mouth and throat; facial neuralgia—pain in the
maxillary joints—acute cutting pains in the cavity of the chest, im-
peding respiration; stitches and tearing in the pectoral muscles; palpitation of the heart, with a sense of anguish; stitches about the
heart, with oppression and sense of congestion; pulsation of the ca-
rotids; gastralgia; colic, with diarrhœa; urgency to urinate, with
increased secretion of sour urine; pains in the region of the kidneys;
tearing, rheumatic-like pains about the clavicles, in the back, the fore-
arm, the shoulders, the neck, which hinder the motion of the head; in
the elbow joints and wrists, in the ligaments of the finger joints, in
the forearms; fleeting stitches in the hips; suddenly stitching tearing
pains in the loins; tearing in the thigh, in the patellæ, in the knee
joints, with swelling thereof, in the shin bone, the calves, the ankles,
the toes and the tendines Achillis. These pains are accompanied with
weariness, heaviness and incapability of moving the affected parts, &c.

According to the results of these provings, Colchicum describes the
sphere of operation of the cause of sero-exudative inflammations, so-
called, with partial implication of the mucous membranes and paralytic-
like sensations, which accompany the pains in the extremities. That
is thus the sphere of the effect of the cause of the so-called arthritic
and muscular rheumatism, or even of the sequelæ of gout.

From the foregoing, we can now fully understand the embarrassment
of the school as regards its indication of Colchicum, because it has no
differential diagnosis between gout and rheumatism.

§ 58.

No doubt can ever arise in Homœopathy regarding *such* a differential diagnosis between two or more spontaneous diseases. It can utterly dispense with it, and, on that very account, evidently, is all the less mistaken in its indications; for it is the same thing to her whether one calls the case in hand gout or rheumatism, because she does not connect her indications with the name of any disease in order to find a remedy which operates against the form in which it appears; but she combines with one of her objects of comparison, that is, with the form of the disease in hand, its objects of comparison from the drug provings, in order to obtain therefrom a sphere of remedial action similar to the pathological form in hand, thus to have an essential indication for a radical cure, i.e., a cure sure, rapid and agreeable to the patient.

Hence, Homœopathy never gives Colchicum in a case corresponding in form, for example, to the proving of Benzoic acid and, vice versa, because an indication, according to natural law, would not thereby be given, and every attempt at a cure would be necessarily frustrated; however, the school knows nothing of these distinctions, and can obtain, consequently, no certain pre-determined results, as its adherents themselves confess. Owing to this confession being true, it is as little qualified to practice as the herdsman. To those who consider this remark rather too severe, I can furnish practical evidence enough of it from daily experience.

§ 59.

Homœopathy reaches still farther with its comprehensive experience. There is, for example, a Rheumatism which corresponds with the pathogenetic results of Bryonia, another corresponding in form with those of Rhus. But, in comparing them with a given case of that disease, these two results are quite often, again, similar to each other, so that often only a single symptom in the form of that disease suffices to decide as regards the essential indication. Here, moreover, the indication may be properly established by observing, whether the pains of the patient occur during rest or motion, since, in the former case, Rhus is indicated, in the latter Bryonia; for it is clear that a great difference must exist in the fact whether the changed functions occur in the organic equipoise of rest or in that of motion.

This law of proportional oscillation which controls, not only the structure of the human body, but, also, its functions, is very influential in Therapeutics, although the school knows nothing of it. According to this law, the whole of the organic mutual action, as indeed its name indicates, can never remain at the same time in equipoise of rest and motion, but some functions rest while the others are more active, or the function itself alternates between rest and motion. Otherwise, the mutual relation of burden and force in the movements of organic substances would be impossible; the organism would wear itself out in the shortest time.

As many physiological laws first present themselves in a clear light in a pathological state of the organism, so does even this. It contains, at the same time, not only the *law of the crisis*, which the physiological school, in its simplicity, reckons among pathological processes; it is, also, the reason why forms of disease exist which are aggravated, now in rest and now in motion, and *vice versa*.

Is not the discovery of such discriminating reasons for Therapeutics of itself a glorious proof of the immense superiority of Homœopathy over the doctrines of physiological medicine?

§ 60.

Since nothing can be understood by itself and nothing can be measured by itself, I must continue to notice the list of our opponents' sins.

The curative method taught in the Universities, rests simply upon the overpowering *of the organic functions which have remained healthy;* it is directed against the law of function, while the law of nutrition is not in the least thought of in this therapeia. In treating the sick, instead of sparing the parts remaining healthy, at any price, its only aim is to give diaphoretics, laxatives, emetics, resolvents, narcotics, alterants, temperants, anti-phlogistics, anti-arthritics, &c., &c.

Yet, if one had but the faintest idea of the law of proportional oscillation, by virtue of which the organism, if disturbed in its state of equipoise, as regards its normal motions of function and nutrition, returns to the same again after the cessation of such processes; that, e.g. after purgation, constipation ensues again, just as after any other excessive irritation of the functions their relaxation sets in—a state of rest which produces anew the functional tension—; then he would not maintain, that if the organism delayed to meet any unreasonable demand made upon it, one had to proceed against it boldly, i.e., with larger doses; a proceeding by which the organic equipoise of rest and motion in the functions would be utterly upset, and, for a long time, perhaps for ever, destroyed.

This presents another reason why, for the medical treatment of this school, no defense can be offered.

§ 61.

It has already been mentioned, in passing, that the indication, from the guiding maxim of the law of similarity, is rewarded by the deductive confirmation, by the appearance of the results previously proclaimed.

Out of these observations grew the experience of Homœopathy, that is, so far as experience can lay claim to validity, only then, when the facts discovered are brought into dependent connection with the laws of nature governing and explained by them.

Upon such experiences the therapeutic schemes of Homœopathy are based, according to the law of the *remembrance* of similar causes, which is not to be confounded with the *expectation* of similar causes, from *habit*, to be met with only in the physiological school.

This scheme lies chiefly in the field of perception, by which I not only recognize again a specific pathological form, but, also, in, and with it, the corresponding unit of comparison, its *homoion pathos* from the drug provings. From the scheme of the specific form of the organism I recognize, at the same time, whether and when the cure has been completed according to the presupposition of the *simile*, i.e., according to the law of similarity.

§ 62.

Thus Homœopathy came into possession of a *general* therapeia, by virtue of which it can, also, assign a number of remedies to general, nosological names, never peremptorily, however, but only conditionally. In a similar manner, it is true, the physiological school *collects* a so-called special therapeutics.

If, however, Homœopathy, under the pathological forms, for instance, under the head of "Gout," presents, among other remedies belonging to this genus, Benzoic acid, also, and Colchicum, vid. §§ 49 and 57, it does not remember, thus, single effects of these substances, but the *whole* scheme of their quality, which is wont to arise from its (combination) with the organism and which the drug-provings discovered in order to complete the synthetic comparison according to the law of similarity. Hence, by the remedies arranged under such a head, we merely mean to say, that they are useful only in those special cases with which the result of the proving agrees in form, by which all room for doubt is removed.

Thus, for every homœopathic indication, the known quantities, the units composed of several parts, which the drugs form in their combination with the organism, are determined beforehand. Were these units not known. then, since as otherwise every individual form of disease itself would represent an *unknown* quantity, every attempt at a cure would be an absurdity, for, from two unknown quantities, a third can not be learned.

It is true, we see, even in the so-called special therapeutics of physiological medicine, under the *general* forms of disease, which moreover it designates as the *special* also, various remedies named *against* them; but only in the sense of expecting similar events according to probability, without any further basis. Thus if their physicians should have to choose between the indications of even but two such remedies, for instance, in Gout, between Benzoic acid and Colchicum, they would, if they were conscientious, die before they came to a decision; for, with them, drugs, in their relation to the human organism, are still utterly unknown quantities. as the Materia Medicas of the physiological school sufficiently prove.

In opposition to this school, Homœopathy, notwithstanding its acquisition according to natural law, does not claim that it possesses a special Therapeia; for the specialties of morbid forms are endless and refuse to be arranged according to any scheme. For special cases, Homœopathy always uses its drug provings, and the arranging of its drugs under general ideas of diseases has, with it, only the significance of an indication for the synthetic comparison still necessary in the special case.

The use of the drug provings, in this manner, does not require any pedantry, which has but little confidence in its own judgment, but rather subjects the same to the guardianship of given words which have to supply the place of nature's laws.

§ 63.

Hence, in Homœopathy, even the examination of the patient takes its cue from the drug provings. If, as is well proven, the diseased human organism always presents a specifically changed form of the *whole* of the immediate reciprocal action of its substances. then the aim of diagnosis can always be directed only to this *whole* and not to any separated part, according to arbitrary teleological conclusions. Hence, it examines, not merely according to anatomical localities, systems and functions, but chiefly according to one or the other, scheme of its drug provings. It takes the entire object of disease as the unit of comparison and not single prominent symptoms, the

purely incidental predicates of the whole. A gouty patient, for instance, calls to mind the various units of comparison which have
shown, in the drug provings, groups of symptoms similar to this
genus; such as Sulphur, Calcarea carb., Aconite, Phosphor. Guai-
acum, Rhus tox., &c., &c., and one versed in Homœopathy seldom
needs a long wearisome comparison, because, in Homœopathy, besides
the technique of the experiment, there is, also, a technique of the
intellect, a subject which I admit, is not heard spoken of in the
clinics of the physiological school.

§ 64.

In fever and ague, for instance, no one is more prompt and ready
with diagnosis and indication than the physiological school. For
the latter, the Indians recommended Quinine to them; Arsenic it
learned to use from the Homœopaths; from analogy with the bitter
taste of quinine, chemistry furnished them the bitter alkaloids;
without considering, however, that such analogies, taken from the
category of quality, to say nothing of the prognosis necessary,
according to modality, have nothing to do with the reciprocal action
of the organism with those qualities. In brief, one or the other remedy
must help, or else, they say, art has no further resources, just as if all
art and all knowledge were at home in this school and not rather a
great lack thereof.

The only differences which the school has discovered as regards
fever and ague, consist in this, that the attacks come sometimes every
day, sometimes every other day, sometimes on the third or fourth day,
now with, now without enlargement of the spleen &c., yet, should any
one ask one of the clinicians of this school about the bearing of such
discriminations upon its therapeutics, he has usually no answer; he
only knows that quinine must be given in doses of from 20 to 60 grs.
i.e. that the dose must be increased, if the cure is tardy. Therefore,
he does not find out that he has done too much, before the patient has
become dropsical or consumptive. For no single one of its therapeutic-
al procedures has this unfortunate school a principle conforming to the
laws of nature, nay, not even a maxim of that kind.

§ 65.

The specific form of fever and ague, which is effectively cured by
Quinine, is not known to this school, because it lacks the logical and
scientific maxims (conforming to natural law) to find it. It is that
quotidian or tertian form, accompanied with swelling and sensitive-

ness of the liver and spleen, with chilliness, without thirst, which does not appear till after the fever, and as soon as the sweat sets in. Hence Quinine cures no fever and ague in which liver and spleen are not swollen; it cures no fever and ague which is characterized during the attack merely, by chilliness, without any subsequent fever and sweat; none with dropsical swellings; also no recent case with burning, unquenchable thirst, during the fever, and without subsequent sweat; yet Quinine, in large doses can *suppress* the attacks of most forms of fever and ague and, by its long continued use, may beget new and far more dangerous diseases and deceive the physician of that category with the semblance of a cure.

§ 66.

Homœopathy proceeds, with far greater security, in its curative efforts. It is guided simply and solely by the existing laws of nature, and chiefly by the laws of nutrition and function : it declines to sacrifice its patients to the mere opinions of others, which can give no guarantee for anything. Hence, in Homœopathy there are no authorities. Here nature's law is the only authority. At first Homœopathy had at its service only the empiric indication of *Hahnemann*, the *simile*, i.e. the law of similarity and thus, for a long time, that law remained, but an empirical rule for therapeutics. Nevertheless, by itself alone even, it led to the most beautiful and brilliant cures, to which all the other history of medicine can present nothing analogous.

The progress of Homœopathy consists in its rationality, acquired after *Hahnemann's* day.

A rational perception differs from an empiric, by this, that it can not only explain its objects by the laws of nature, but also that the laws of nature themselves are re-confirmed by these objects.

Thus, what, for a long time, had no other validity in Homœopathy, but that of an *empiric maxim*, developed, in the course of subsequent studies, into a rational system.

The *simile* was a logical comparative formula from relative ideas, at least according to the meaning of the words by which Hahnemann has expressed it; the possible and actual were formerly determined merely according to the rule of logical comparative ideas, in the same manner as it was done, with regard to the *Contrarium*.

§ 67.

But if one wishes to use comparative ideas, he must, at least express them in a precise manner, and, then, "like" means that which agrees according to the cause; "similar" that which agrees according to form, and "contrary" that which agrees neither as to form nor cause.

Since now no organ, no cell-complex, and no cell consists of *one* substance only, so also the pathological increase or diminution or change of any kind of one or more substances of the same organ, in comparison with artificially produced diseases of the same parts, can always make itself known only by similar or contrary, but never by the same functions and their consequences. The former occurs when we proceed according to the laws of reciprocal action, and do not, according to the causal law, over-excite one function or another, a proceeding according to which, of course, a double, threefold, &c., quantity of a substance will produce a double, threefold, &c., motion.

All phenomena in nature as we know, may, as regards their last cause, be referred back, to the laws of motion. If opium, for example, in small quantity excites the nervous system, then an accelerated motion is communicated by the former to the latter, whereupon the inexperienced cries out, *opium excitat!* In increased quantities, however, it does not excite any more, on the contrary, every motion is by a twofold or threefold quantity of opium, so *oppressed* that the school can say also, *opium sedat!* Thereby, however, no rest in the equipoise of motion is expressed as in ₰ 59, but an over-excitement, an overthrow of function.

As regards these relative ideas, I must give another familiar example:

There is an inflammation of the last digital phalanx, a panaritium (or felon) from external injury, and another from the consequences, still continuing in the interior of the organism, owing to external causes. As regards the locality, even, the two resemble each other, but they are neither alike nor opposite. Now, Homœopathy, among other remedies, for panaritium, has two drugs, viz: Ledum palustre and Silicia. Each of these, taken internally, causes a similar inflammation; but, as regards the form of the inflammation, they are neither alike nor opposite. The administration of these two substances to the sick had established the fact that Silicia is one of the remedies which can cure panaritium in all its stages, when it is the consequence of the permanent results of external causes, but not when arising from external injury. As regards Ledum palustre, the same clinical use showed that, on the contrary, it cures the panaritium produced by external injury, and that only in the first stage. If mortification has set in, it can be checked only by arsenic; while the physiological school, in both cases, passively waits for spontaneous exarticulation, or has to

proceed to amputation, which, in the latter case, cannot always avert a fatal result.

<h2 style="text-align:center">§ 68.</h2>

We know, however, that Silicia is found in the bones, and one of the first forms of panaritium has its seat in the periphery of the bone of the last joint of the finger. Hence, it is fair to assume that the Silicia, in the one case, shall manifest itself as a nutrition-remedy, and the Ledum, in the other, as a function-remedy; therefrom we may infer that the nutritive and functional, i.e., the empiric basis of the cure can never be explained by the *Simile*, while, at the same time, the *Simile* remains the only basis, according to natural law, for an indication in all cases, in which no medicine, deductively confirmed by its use upon the sick, exists; which use, however, from reasons to be given hereafter, can, in no case, be injurious. Consequently, even in such cases in which there is scarcely any more than *one* symptom present, the Simile may claim to be the basis conformable to natural law.

Thus the Simile is and remains, not only the only maxim of indication, but, also, the only *mine* for the discovery of new remedies—an acquisition from which the physiological school is, as yet, as far removed as from all therapeutic laws, which are chiefly to be found only in Homœopathy.

<h2 style="text-align:center">§ 69.</h2>

Something great must fill us with admiration, even by the most insignificant parts of its spheres. There is hardly any disease which seems more trivial to the physiological school than just this very panaritium; one can, at the most, only lose a finger-joint! For this reason let me mention purposely still another form of this disease.

If a physician of the physiological school is called to a patient, the end of whose finger is swollen about the nail, deep red and very painful, with the formation of pus evident at the root of the nail, he will open it without delay and poultice it, because he thinks that all felons are run in the same mould. Beyond that he does not know what to do. But now the suppuration spreads, penetrates the phalangal joint and appears upon the inner side of the finger. That gives him another opportunity of making, even there, a deep and long incision, through which, at length, the whole bone of the joint, which, in the meantime, has become dead, must be removed.

Homœopathy teaches a different process. Its physicians inquire, at once, after the circumstances accompanying the felon; and if it is found, for example, that the patient looks sick and pale, and, in the morning, feels dull and confused in his head; if he complains of loss of appetite and, in the evening, of chilliness and heat; if he says that the pains in the finger are more endurable in the open air than in the room; hence, if, in consequence of this, the physicians examine the room and find that the walls are very damp—what else, in such a case, shall the physician of the physiological school be able to do, but to poultice and lance, in spite of the frequent unfavorable results of this treatment?

. If the Homœopathic physicians find, however, that, some days after, a blister appears upon another finger of the same patient, which had previously remained healthy, and, if they ask whether the patient, also, observed such a water-blister on that part of the finger first affected, and are answered in the affirmative; the physician of the physiological school, notwithstanding this anamnesis, will still not know what else to do than to poultice and lance as soon as possible.

The former physicians, however, would be led, by these accompanying circumstances, to the provings of Natrum sulph.; they would give it in the third decimal attenuation and both fingers would be well in a few days, as I can confirm from my own practice. Such cases are cured neither by poultice nor lancing; neither, as I have myself experienced, by Ledum, Arsenic nor Silicea.

§ 70.

With far less trouble than it needs to acquire such knowledge, the physician of the physiological school throws all such facts into the category of inconceivabilities, hence, according to his mental capacity of association, even under that of impossibilities. He moreover, ridicules the idea of thinking that a felon could be cured by Natrum sulph., by a salt which is nothing but a very prompt purgative! He does not know that every error is a conclusion from *effect to cause*, which lacks the inductive proof. Upon this point he is the strongest among all opponents. In this he obeys the same law of the lower course of thought to which men were formerly accustomed when they thought that the stars were nailed fast in the firm arch of Heaven, and hence experienced the greatest difficulty to conceive of them as floating unsuspended in different positions. These ancestors of ours had as little right, as those adherents of the physiological school, to consider the limitation of their capacities as a limitation inherent in the bodies of nature, with regard to the kinds of existences and mutual motions possible. Moreover, one could maintain, with the same right, that it was inconceivable, hence, impossible, that the same sunlight should bleach wax and blacken chloride of silver, because the same cause could not have different effects. Hence, on the same ground on which the fox in the fable declared the sweet grapes sour, he makes *merry* over Homœopathic cures and denies them *in toto*. Quite naturally! for as a member of the Faculty, he would, by a concession, have to deprive himself of just the praise which he would bestow upon Homœopathic cures.

Concerning his diagnosis, viz,—to pay attention to the accompanying circumstances, as well as to those under which improvement or aggravation takes place, he does not only neglect them, but he gets angry, also, when the complaints of the patients trouble him with matters for which he has no re-agents—no pleximeter, no stethoscope, &c.; and the instruments of thought, which would help him out of the trouble, seem to him like the accidental reasons why some creatures pray to the moon and others bark at it. Hence, it is, also, impossible for him to discover a law of nature, or to grasp the substance and reach of one already known, because such subjects can not be discovered and known by grasping, but only by thinking.

§ 71.

Not only in felons, but, in very many other cases, Homœopathy has taken the knife for ever out of the hand of surgery, the knife which is so often mischievous and unnecessary, though much easier to handle than a remedy; this is an infinitely rich gain for suffering humanity which may be already calculated by the fact that Homœopathy surely cures enchondroma, caries, carcinoma, polypus, many forms of cataract, many benign and malignant tumors, &c., especially in the earlier stages. In Homœopathy, too, the occurrence of tetanus, or pyæmia, after operations, puerperal fever, &c., is to be reckoned among the greatest rarities, while, at the same time, it makes Chloroform quite superfluous in childbirth, and styptics, too, for the most part.

These views are looked upon with all the more disfavor by the adherents of the physiological school, inasmuch as these two branches, Surgery and Midwifery, form, in modern times, the only welcome refuge for these physicians; for when they have nothing to puncture, to cut, to operate on or tie up, they are ill at ease, since according to their own confession they are without any reliable therapeia whatever. If any one indulges, however, in the most distant and delicate allusion to this fact, they have no proof to the contrary, but seek to repulse such unpleasantnesses with insolence or fly into a passion—tokens of the disturbed condition of the mind on account of the unwilling loss of something of great value.

. "Envy !—You never can appease it !
Hence, only ridicule and tease it !"

§ 72.

Panaritium, being, for the adherents of Physiological medicine, one of the most insignificant diseases, because its treatment is made as short as possible, and consists simply in poulticing and cutting, I have chosen it as an example, setting forth, in a very simple manner, their whole therapeutic aim, which simply applies remedies in order *to experiment upon the results of diseases,* as if the cause were always removed with the results ; while, as we have shown, the field of homœopathic therapeutics comprises the causes and conditions of diseases, and is the only field from which the sources of essential indication, for a rational therapeia, can spring.

We have already seen four remedies for the felon, arising from this source, and yet the special therapeia, for the various forms under which the insignificant felon may appear, is far from ended : on the contrary, to complete the special therapeia for any genus of disease is quite as impossible as to describe all men, of all times, because the conditions of disease change with time. Nevertheless, every therapeutics, worthy of being called rational, ought to *stand prepared also, for all future cases, as yet unknown,* which can only be done by a general pathology a nd therapeia based upon natural laws, such as Homœopathy possesses.

I saw for example, the last described panaritium, neither in the Hospitals of Berlin, Munich or Vienna, nor in my own practice of many years, nor did I ever hear or read of it, during that whole time ; only during the last year nature presented to me seven cases of the kind.

Who will warrant that, at some other time, in some other place, under other circumstances, some other forms of felon may not occur, and where should physiological medicine find the remedies for such conditions if it would not study the homœopathic drug provings,and what belongs thereto, whereby it would obtain all information for all cases, and these drug provings are daily growing in material ? It knows indeed, that the so called genius of a disease changes from time to time, but its teachers, its professors and clinicians, do not know how, for their therapeutics would also have to be changed thereby. For this reason, none of them, for the last half century, have furnished anything practical and of lasting value in therapeutics; for, what proved to be practical, came only from practical physicians, among whom, *Hahnemann* and *Rademacher* hold the highest place, but who are not understood by these professors and clinicians.

§ 73.

For many years past, it is true, even physiological medicine has occupied itself with drug provings, not on men, however, but on frogs, rabbits and various domestic animals, and from these experiments it ventures to form inferences with regard to the human organism. We shall expose these fallacies and dismiss them with an example.

The school, for example forms the following syllogism: 1. Jalapa vomits dogs. 2. Man vomits too, Ergo 3. Jalapa vomits man. That is such a syllogism as; The earth has inhabitants: the moon is an earth: therefore the moon has inhabitants.

Both are false. The first may be shown false by experiment, since the dog, even when the œsophagus is tied, gets no diarrhœa, after large doses of Jalapa, while man, as a general thing, gets diarrhœa, and, only exceptionally vomiting. Hence the school arranges Jalapa not among the emetics but the cathartics.

The fallacy in both instances lies in this, that, in a categorical syllogism the first premise must give the general; the second, must subordinate the particular to the general; the third must determine the particular from the general; this, however, is not the case in the previous instances.

If the school could say, "The dog is a man; Jalapa vomits the dog, Hence, it must vomit a man," it would all have been proper. But the general, the sphere of the canine organism, is not that of the human.

Experiments on animals can, at the most, only furnish us with analogous confirmations of the Homœopathic drug provings, but no new or available *inductions* and indications for therapeutics.

Hence, no one could refuse to agree with *Liebig*, if he had not referred to Homœopathy, but only to physiological medicine, when he says, in Vol. 1, p. 105 of his "Chemischen Briefe," "Truly one would be led to think, that, among the sciences which have for their object the knowledge of Nature and its forces, Medicine should take the lowest place as an *inductive* science;" for indeed there are no inductive conclusions in physiological medicine, and were even an opportunity offered to it to show the creative power of induction, it prefers to cling to explanations set forth by the physicians of a former age. §48.

Posology.

§ 74.

Finally, I must speak of the *Dose*, one of the greatest discoveries of Homœopathy, and, for physiological medicine, the most incomprehensible that ever existed.

The *Simile* is, in its practicability, inconceivable and impossible, if no regard is paid to the quantity of the dose.

As regards the dose, the *Simile* is guided exclusively by the relation which exists between the quantities of the substances and forces of the organism and the quantity of morbific matter. The law of dose can, after what has been said, be deduced only from the fundamental maxim of the *relativity of all motion*. No other guiding maxim for the discovery and determination of the rational dose of the indicated drug is to be had, because it is the only one based upon natural law.

We also know, from the preceding, that the quality, and with it also, the quantity, of a drug must, of necessity describe the same orbit of action within the organism as the morbific cause; for we can not, for example, expect that Rhubarb will dilate the pupils and Belladonna move the bowels; that Quinine will produce sleep, nor opium cure fever and ague. It is, the *quality* which *localizes* the quantity in the organism. For these reasons, the quantity of the dose must accordingly subordinate itself to the quality, and, from the law of the equivalence of forces, we know that the action and counter-action, which a drug should produce, need not be any greater than the morbific cause: moreover that the intensity of disease, arises not alone from the quantity of the cause but mostly from its quality. Since, finally, diseases are nothing but changes in the physiological substances of nutrition and function, and their forces, produced by some morbific matter, so the *law of nutrition* is our chief dependence for determining the quantity of the *dose*.

§ 75.

If, in the blood corpuscles, for instance, we find 1,186 per ct. of chlorine: 0,066 per ct. of sulphuric acid; 0,134 per ct. of phosphoric acid; 3,323 per ct. of potash; 1,341 per ct. of Soda; 0,114 per ct. of phosphate of lime; 0,073 per ct. talcose earth, we can, in opposition to the physiological school, not hope to communicate with advantage, to the movements of the diseased organism, such substances in a larger per centage *per dose*; on the contrary, we must administer still smaller quantities, on account of the necessary repetition of the dose.

But it is in vain that nature speaks so distinctly to the opponents of Homœopathy. They do not even listen with sufficient intelligence to remind themselves of their own Liebig. According to Liebig, for instance, the duckweed takes up only 16 per ct. of the 35 per ct. of lime dissolved in the water: only 5 per ct. of the 12 per ct. of Magnesia : only 5 per ct. of the 10 of common salt; however, notwithstanding that but 3 per ct. of potash and 0,721 per ct. of oxide of Iron, combined with traces of Alumina, are dissolved in water, it takes up of the former 12 per ct. and, of the latter, 7, 135 per ct. This it evidently does, not arbitrarily, but according to the laws of its specification, by virtue of which, it can take up neither more nor less of these substances for its nutrition and function, or to, take an example from Zoology, we know that the pearl oyster forms its shell in a water poor in lime ; in a water richer in lime, it ceases to appropriate the lime and dies. In view of this, should the dogma of the Universities that " Much helps much," restrain the practical physician from conducting himself according to such laws of nature and compel him to oppose, to the motions of the organism, substances of the outer world by the grain, scruple, drachm, or ounce, and should it be allowed to teach him to cure the sick accordingly ?

§ 76.

From the law that substances act upon each other only by their surfaces, we know further that everything which produces an intimate contact of substances, increases their affinity and repulsion. Hence it is clear that we must, as much as possible, transfer drugs from their massive into their molecular state, by attenuation and trituration, so that the single molecules may become separated and isolated and thus be able to enter into the most intimate contact possible with the molecules of organic substances. Actual proof of this is given in the letter preceding this essay.

§ 77.

As regards the practical application of the Simile to the sick, it is, upon the maturest consideration, necessary to administer the remedies in a quantity or dose as minute and imponderable as are the quantities of the morbific causes. Now has any one ever weighed the quantity of the substance which produces Scarlet fever, Measles, Intermittent fever &c ? and why does the physiological school, in vaccination, use imponderable quantities only, in order to check the movements of the small-pox virus, in its combination with the organism, and not use the same imponderable quantities also for the cure of other diseases? Because even in this, it is not guided by any law of nature, but only by an empirical accident. Empiricism, that school comprehends, but the law of nature is, to it incomprehensible.

§ 78.

Besides, the physiological school still fondly remains in a great error regarding the qualities of the homœopathic attenuations in general. It maintains, for instance, that when we add to 100 drops of water or alcohol, ten drops of any drug in fluid form, to prepare a solution, the number of drops then increases to 110.

But it has been a known fact in chemistry for a long time, that, with the combination of water with alcohol, or, its solution in water, a condensation ensues, so that the volume is less, after the solution, than the sum of the volumes of the constituents of the solution. Surely this fact ought to have offered sufficient inducement to inquire whether it was probable that similar motions took place in homœopathic attenuations, before wasting time in useless calculations, incorrect premises, from which to conclude that the homœopathic attenuations, as to their material contents, were like a drop in the ocean. The truth, however, is quite different. Even water consists of hydrogen and oxygen and, hence, every molecule of water possesses the same chemical constitution. The like holds good with regard to solutions of salts; according to Dr. Jolly, "It can not be doubted that solution is accomplished by the mutual attraction between the water and the salt, otherwise, by reason of its greater specific gravity, the salt would fall to the bottom. The attraction which manifests itself only under contact-proximity and which is hence molecular attraction, begets an approximation of the points acting upon each other, till, finally, that distance is reached, in which the repulsion, which increases with the approximation of the points, is in equipoise with the molecular attraction.

" Consequently, if there is an attraction between the molecules of the solvent, and of the body dissolved, then an approximation of these points ensues, hence a contraction. The amount of the contraction, occurring with the progress of attenuation, gives the measure of the attraction still present, with the increasing distances."

§ 79.

These principles form inductive conclusions which Jolly was compelled to draw from his experiments. He experimented with solutions of saltpetre and found that, when he added 1257.8 cc of water to a solution of 1000 cc a contraction of 21.26 cc took place, just as if, in consequence of this mixture, those 21 cc, according to a comparison with the sums of the constituents used for it, were now missing—had been lost.

The co-efficient of condensation, naturally, decreases steadily, with the increase of attenuation ; yet, with an attenuation of the same solution with 4327.6 cc more water, there occurred a further condensation of the total mass of 15 cc, and, finally, when other 24311.6 cc of water were added, the condensation still amounted to 13 cc.

§ 80.

If we consider that, according to calculation, even this last contraction is equal to the pressure of eight atmospheres, and the weight of the column of quicksilver in the barometer is equal to the pressure of one atmosphere, then the efficiency of the molecules of such attenuations, upon the organism, can no longer be disputed, and indeed may be assumed for far higher attenuations.

Simply to deny the efficiency of *any homœopathic attenuation whatever*, is not admissible as long as these experiments have not been completed with regard to all substances. Not till a condensation can be no longer observed, and the attenuation has been carried so far that all its molecules are *homogeneous*, can they be declared to be inefficient.

Before this inefficiency is *confirmed* by experiment, we must consider, even as regards our organism, every molecule of a substance, set free by attenuations, as the product of its volume into its density, according to which the forces, specifically belonging to it, offer resistance to its inorganic surrounding, till, overpowered, it is resolved into its atoms. Hence we can not transfer, in case of homœopathic attenuations the views regarding the unattenuated bodies concerning the coherence of their masses, and mutual relations, to the molecules of bodies set free by these attenuations.

Hence in shaking the attenuations and in triturating solid bodies, it is our aim to obtain surfaces and forces, for forces are nothing but the properties of bodies. Moreover no one maintains that Homœopathy would or could transfer forces to inert vehicles, to alcohol, water or sugar of milk, without a simultaneous transfer of the matter from which those forces issue. Those, however, who believe that, even in this, they have discovered something repugnant to sound reason, may have the goodness to prove it.

§ 81.

It will be a long time before the latest discoveries in the very domain of chemistry even, will be able to purge the prevailing abderitism from its mental association with massive doses. By reference to the preceding letter, *Bunsen's and Kirchhoff's Spectral Analysis* has presented to the naked eye less than the $\frac{1}{3,000,000}$ of a milligramme of Soda. These are then the smallest quantities which can be made apparent to our sense of vision, and, when bodies still exist in such infinite subdivision, then their forces must also act. What other argument, based upon natural law, can yet be presented against the powerful efficiency of the attenuations generally used in Homœopathy? Only the most disgusting prudery would any longer maintain such trifling opposition against this system.

The doctrine of molecular bodies and their forces will, with irresistible force, break through the stagnation of the chemistry of the present day. Chemistry, which has pretended to be the possessor of all knowledge, has in the face of such reactions, thus far had nothing to show but crude experiments, which lacked the living ray of thought, and which passed from hand to hand, like mummies adorned with halos. Therefore, since chemistry has attained to that point where authority becomes stationary, it will surely neglect also to subject itself to the laws of nature, till the profounder study of the molecules and their forces, shall have overthrown the previous boundaries of chemical ideas. Then it will look with amazement at the laws of Homœopathy, just as the Indian archer does at the revolver. When it finally shall have recovered from its astonishment of many years, then the prevalent false medical doctrines, taught in the Universities, will come, at last, to an inglorious end.

If now the lines in the spectrum are produced by a chemical property of the bodies, which is of a nature as unchangeable and fundamental as the atomic weight of matter, if the unheard of sensibility of these reactions permits of the dilution even of the $\frac{1}{3,000,000}$ of a milligramme of Chloride of Sodium or the $\frac{6}{1,000,000}$ of Strontium &c.: then Chemistry may easily demonstrate the material contents of homœopathic attenuations, and it must do it before it ventures again to assail, with arbitrary opinions, the experiments of Homœopathy, which long ago has far outstripped it.

The so-called exact sciences are now obliged to shuffle after Homœopathy; the nimbus of the balance has vanished; the tangible has

53

been abandoned and the experiment has been directed *to the great forces of the smallest masses.*

The criterion of a science conformable to natural law rests upon this, that no new discovery can overthrow it; on the contrary, can only confirm it. Hence, whatever has been set forth against Homœopathy was naught but fancy, for, with every new discovery of natural sciences, it roots firmer and deeper; though Homœopathic literature swarms with unsuccessful attempts to explain facts presented to it upon its own domain, yet none of its fundamental principles are antiquated, but all have remained new and have grown as regards root, trunk. branch and fruit.

§ 82.

Now if we should ask one of these clinicians who think themselves so very learned, and who look down upon Homœopathy with such contempt, what cured his fever and ague patient, for example, to whom he had given Quinine, since the daily dose of Quinine taken in full weight, was found in the urine of the patient, he would be unable to answer. If even his vaccinations did not suffice to direct him to the laws of Homœopathy, such experiments as these, at any rate, should lead him to think deeper than the causal law reaches.

The laws of nutrition and function teach us that Quinine is no nutrition remedy, hence can not be made available for growth, and the laws of organic hyloteretic processes demonstrate, that, in the cure of such a fever and ague, it is not the ponderable quantities of Quinine that we have to do with, but the imponderable molecules.

The clinician does not know, as yet, the maxim of the frugality of nature, in obedience to which the number of fundamental principles is not to be increased unnecessarily, for just as Virchow according to § 48, needlessly enlarges the idea of metastasis, without being reproved by his adherents. since they have no antennae for such errors, so, without hesitation, the whole school of physiological medicine stands by the old proposition; as in a machine, thus also in diseases, will a large quantity of medicine act to a better advantage than a smaller?

In this it sins against the law of the relativity of all motions which not only renders this proposition superfluous, but also characterizes it as utterly false, and thus it is at the same time, demonstrated that it unnecessarily increases the number of fundamental principles for the doctrine of the dose.

§ 83.

There are chemists who say; granted even that any efficacy could be ascribed to Homœopathic attenuations, as such, yet the substances which they contain, in consequence of such an infinite separation of their molecules. must necessarily be changed by the alkaline saliva or the acid gastric juice and, for this very reason, lose all efficacy.

This is an utterly one sided inference, from the category of modality, such as the astronomers drew, at the time when Galileo invented the telescope, remarking as they did: "How, is it possible, that Jupiter could have four moons, since we can not see them with our eyes, and how can a wooden tube, with a bit of glass at both ends, make them apparent, even *granting* that they are really there."

It seems as if these chemists had lost confidence in their own reason the moment they hear of any fact from Homœopathy, while they express their amazement in quite a different manner over similar and far more surprising events in their own laboratories.

Thus Dr. *Mohr* was not a little astonished, as we learn from his Lehrbuch der chemisch-analytischen Titrirmethode, when, upon introducing carbonic acid into a solution of chloride of calcium in ammonia, this fluid was *not at once* rendered turbid, nor even after a longer time, though carbonic acid, introduced into fluid ammonia, produces at once carbonate of ammonia, and this salt, with the chloride of lime, would precipitate, under all circumstances, carbonate of lime. This is an observation which flies in the face of all chemical ideas, just as the other does, made by the same chemist when he poured caustic soda into water containing carbonic acid and a solution of litmus, and then observed that the soda solution colored every thing perfectly a bright blue, though the red color re-appeared after a time.

It never occurred to him, however, to say, "That is impossible," yet he was obliged to concede that the former phenomenon could not be comprehended according to the usual chemical views, while the latter was very surprising and could not be explained by the facts which science offers us at present.

Facts, however, never explain anything, because they do not themselves judge.

But if those chemists had only proceeded correctly, according to the single scheme of modality, then they would, in order to prove the possible by means of the real, have been obliged, at any rate, to make experiments with Homœopathic attenuations, at the sick bed, whereupon they would have observed that *attenuated* substances manifest a still stronger resistance to their inorganic surroundings (see Grundgesetze, &c., p. 398), and, only when they have passed into the circulation of the blood, do they submit to the movements and laws of the organism.

In fact, the molecules of Homœopathic attenuations, in spite of saliva and the gastric juice, in every newly given case, always produce the same specific counter-actions within the organism; they are not destroyed, even under conditions which must appear to chemistry as very injurious. For the sugar of milk of the pellets, for example, which are saturated with the attenuations of the acids, combines with none of them and is as little changed thereby, as these very acids themselves, since they do not lose, after many years, their specific effect upon the organism. Even the attenuated vegetable substances, in the pellets, do not lose their specific action, though they are often put up in paper containing chlorine. The attenuated Iodine does not combine with the starchy contents of the globules which it saturates; even the attenuated nitrate of silver no longer suffers from exposure to light; the attenuated sulphur ceases to combine with the silver of the spoon by which it is given, nor can even the lime in the spring water, in which Homœopathic attenuations are usually administered, enter into any combination with the attenuated substances, which, in any other condition, would be instantly changed by them, &c., &c.

Had those wise chemists only subjected their inference to the category of relation, before they ventured to raise those objections to the efficacy of Homœopathic attenuations, they would have found, that, in fact, and as is generally well known, neither the saliva, nor the acid of the stomach is able to change the separate molecules of our food, though they are in close contact with it for a long time, consequently the molecules of iron, of lime, of potash, in short, of all the molecular substances of our food are carried, in safety, to every part of the organism where they are needed, and that the case can not be at all different with the molecules of drugs.

Let chemistry persist in denying such facts if it please so to do, and if it has not the faculty of believing them, but it would be wiser if it would refrain from touching these Homœopathic experiences, as Dr. Mohr refrained from touching his, until it shall have succeeded, in comprehending them. That would be rational at least. In Chemistry it is true, any assertion may be presented as an acceptable one, since, as yet, it has no principle, and lacks any basis whatever for maintaining or rejecting any, outside of experiment.

But this is just the curse of empiricism, that it loses the capacity for thinking and reasoning.

The Strategy of our Opponents.

§ 84.

According to the fundamental law of the relativity of all motions, Homœopathy sometimes uses large doses, not indeed with the false notion of thus affecting any cure, but for the sake of palliation and temporary aid, by the removal of obstacles to the cure.

If, for example, the metallic dust of tinsel which floats about in the shops of inlayers is inhaled, producing ulceration of the lungs, it would be repugnant to that law of nature to use, in such and similar metallic poisonings, minute doses. Here, according to the law of causation, even Homœopathy gives the iodide of potash in Allopathic doses, i.e. about half a drachm dissolved in from 4 to 5 ounces of water, 2 or 3 teaspoonfuls to be taken daily. Yet it knows that, with the cause, all the results are not removed, and completes the cure according to the *Simile*.

Thus Homœopathy removes with Castor oil, or its own tincture of Rhubarb &c., any injurious matter in the intestinal canal, the presence of which would hinder the progress of the recovery of a disease, thus complicated, according to the law of *Simile*, e.g. Typhlitis ; or as, in cases of Asthma and other diseases which have become incurable, it relieves with morphine, and neutralizes excess of acid in the stomach, for the time being, with soda. It also administers Quinine, in grain doses, in violent intermittents, well knowing that chiefly during the past year, the most fatal accidents have occurred, as e.g., cerebral intoxication by massive pigment embolism—in order to prevent the copious formation of pigment in the venous caverns of the spleen, and thus to render impossible the truly metastatic, because, mechanical, deposition of these pigmented cells into nobler organs. In so doing however, Homœopathy knows very well that thus it can effect *no cure*, but only a momentary suppression of the formation of the pigment, yet can by no means destroy the cause of that process ; that, moreover, if the use of these quantities of Quinine were persisted in, injurious consequences would be sure to follow, and that the cure itself is only to be attempted in accordance with the *Simile*.

Such auxiliaries, from the causal law, hence from a law of nature, Homœopathy, as a Therapeutics based upon natural law, does not despise, and so far as they are rationally used, one may say that Homœopathy and Allopathy, provided the latter have any rationality, form mutual complements and no direct contrasts.

The difference betwen Allopathy and Homœopathy is here again, that the former, without law or rule, proceeds empirically and besides cherishes the conviction of having effected cures by such procedures, while, on the contrary, the latter takes the above mentioned law of nature, as the only correct rule for its actions at the sick bed. Hence it must be set down in the category of slanders against Homœopathy to maintain, that, in such cases, it knew not how to help itself or that it was rejecting its own therapeutic means.

From § 73, up to this point, the law of dose is determined according to quantity, quality, relation and modality; consequently it contains an impregnable truth and a fundamental law of nature.

§ 85.

To this category of slanders also belongs the assertion that Homœopathy neglects the other diagnostic auxiliaries of auscultation, percussion, microscopy and chemistry. Our opponents again differ from us, in this respect, that they know how to use these auxiliary means merely to make out the diagnosis of a case, while Homœopathy, from these diagnostic auxiliaries, can, at the same time, establish indications for its remedies which reach the minutest details, as we have made apparent, among other things by the example of Aconite and Phosphorus in § 52, for the various stages of pneumonia. As students and beginners, we must always, it is true, appeal for aid to microscopy and chemistry in order to study, for example, the pathological constituents of the urine. Subsequently a practised eye detects the sediments of uric acid, the ammonio-phosphate of Magnesia, epithelia, blood, pus, &c., while the conclusion concerning the presence of albumen, sugar, &c., in the urine can be deduced with certainty at a much earlier date, from the other symptoms, even before chemistry, can detect albumen and sugar in the urine with its reagents.

§ 86.

As regards microscopy, I know of but few cases for which it would be necessary in practice, and even there, as a general thing, it only serves to *confirm* the previously acquired diagnostic knowledge, for instance, the discovery of carbonate of lime in the urine. But to this also the earlier groups of symptoms already invite our attention, as for example, in mental diseases, especially in diseases of the brain and incipient diseases of the bones, atrophy &c.

Moreover, in my large practice of many years, I have used the microscope but twice to establish the diagnosis. One case was that of a man 31 years of age, whose physicians, there were three of them called in council, had treated him six years long for spermatorrhœa and impotence, without result. The cause of their ill success was clear to me, from the fact that the microscopic examination of the secretion showed not a single animalculum and only revealed the large globules of mucus from the prostate. A further examination made in consideration of that observation, showed an enormous hypertrophy of the prostate by which those two morbid phenomena found their explanation. This man sought my help because he was just about to conclude a very advantageous marriage. In this case, of course, demands would have been made upon him which he well knew he was incapable of meeting. Yet, after my diagnosis, he was perfectly cured in six weeks of his impotence and his so called spermatorrhœa : he married and soon after begat a boy. But before one speaks of spermatorrhœa and impotence, he should at any rate examine the prostate, and then, the microscope would be superfluous.

In another case, an acquaintance complained to me of the steadily increasing emaciation of his only little son, who followed several daughters. He was a feudal lord and, hence, this complaint was a vital point for his family. As I was not his physician, I advised the gentleman to direct the attention of his family physician to the milk of the nurse who suckled the child. This was done, and that physician replied that the milk was very good, and that hence, it could not be the cause of the emaciation. I now showed the gentleman, the *Atlas, execute d'apres nature du microscope-daguerreotype de Donne,* where in Fig. 69, woman's milk is depicted, but in Figs. 75, 76 and 77 the Colostrum. He thereupon brought me directly some of the nurse's milk in a vial. A drop was put under the microscope, when he himself recognized the milk, at once as colostrum : he discharged that nurse, and recognized the milk of the new nurse just as readily, under the microscope as the milk of a healthy woman. He retained this nurse; the child gained from day to day and has now become a hearty boy. But, in case of atrophy of children, is it not the first duty to change the food ?

§ 87.

Is it surprising that Homœopathy, which comprises in itself the entire art of diagnosis, prognosis, indication and therapeutics, as far as it is known on this earth, shows the greatest superiority over its opponents? For this also I must adduce one of the many evidences furnished by my practice, a case which has occurred but lately, and corresponds very well with the previous one of gout.

A man 36 years of age had pains in the hip-joint, in the thigh, the knee, the ankle and in the calves, which, after four weeks of allopathic tratment, had extended to all the joints of the body, so that sometimes the patient could move none of them. He had sleepless nights; besides, quantities of medicine deprived him of his appetite and thus, of course, of all his strength. He despaired of his recovery, and since he got worse every week, his friends urged him, so to speak, to change the system. That was done; I found all the joints, those of the spine included, quite immovable, or, at least, restricted in motion, and moved only with pain. After I had finished my homœopathic examination, I promised this patient that he would be able to get up in four days, and, in fourteen days, return to his office. That was an easy thing for me to do. The previous physician had spoken of gout, and, conformably to his standpoint, as an adherent of the physiological school, did not trouble himself about the other accompanying symptoms of the disease and, in fact, had not even inquired about them: for the diagnosis was made out as gout and that was the end of it. From my examination, according to the law of *Simile*, I saw distinctly that I had to do with what the school calls a masked intermittent. As I prognosticated, so it turned out. On the fourth day this patient walked up and down in his room, and, after twenty-one days, in which he had only the damp November weather to guard against, he was in his counting-room.

Let the opponents of Homœopathy say what they may, such cases as these open wide the eyes of the stupidest layman. And what, moreover, even in a general view is to be expected from a doctrine which assumes this boastful title, that of "physiological medicine" a contradiction in terms. Under these circumstances of course, no one will be surprised, if, as it happened in this case, the former physician, on meeting the cured man said. " You had the gout for six weeks, and, since, within that space of time the gout process is wont to run its course, your cure can not be ascribed to Homœopathy."

Such sophisms, to be used with ignorant and credulous laymen, are always ready at hand with our opponents. This cured man, however, ventured to remark, "Most worthy doctor ! had you after making me swallow a fresh bottle of medicine almost every day, under a constant aggravation of my disease, instead of suggesting an electro-magnetic treatment, only said to me. ' You shall get up in four days and in twenty-one days be in your counting room, it would never have entered my head to have sought other advice."

Dust must always be thrown in the face of the public whenever its opponents hear of a homœopathic cure: something else must always have effected it, only not Homœopathy, although they can not possibly believe in the correctness of their own subterfuges and much less can they prove it. To settle the matter, however, it is only necessary to compare the prescriptions of both sides: under such an embarrassment our opponents, who assert that they always stand upon the ground of exact art and science, prefer to turn their backs on all experience and, with the easily deluded laymen, whose patience is often superhuman, to take a stand upon mists and clouds, in order to mislead them by the twilight of their own authority, exalting themselves rather than their own art.

§ 88.

There is still another difference between Homœopathy and Allopathy worthy of consideration. Homœopathic drugs are prepared, in all parts of the world, according to the same directions; the allopathic according to the various directions of the various pharmacopœias in various countries and states. Vegetable sustances are also boiled or scalded or steamed, and, by the influence of heat, many vegetable molecules are changed in their powers.

A chemist understands what it means to work with reagents which are not uniform. It destroys all reliability of his labor, as well as of the data regarding the results obtained.

Since, furthermore, homœopathic molecular substances are beyond the reach of chemical reagents, and their improper preparation can not be discovered till it is shown by their injurious effect upon the diseased organism, the principles of humanity require that the preparation of such remedies should not be entrusted to the most violent of our enemies, the Allopathic druggists, but, with the greatest safety, to Homœopathic physicians themselves, whose whole success depends upon their preparation.

§ 89.

Although nothing can overthrow the laws of nature and the inductive proofs which have been already adduced, showing the possibility and necessity of homœopathic attenuations and triturations for the purpose of healing, yet Homœopathy is sustained by still greater evidence, namely, ocular demonstration, by the *deductive* confirmation of its inductive conclusions at the sick bed.

That Homœopathy is a demonstrative science, and in this respect, among all other sciences, stands nearest to mathematics in certainty, is shown by the regressive syllogisms from effect to the cause, possible only to Homœopathy, i.e. from the cure of a given case to the remedy which produced it, which I trust has been made clear by the foregoing examples of the various forms of intermittent fever.

If the Allopathic, or Physiological, school could only offer a single proof or doctrine which at all approached, in value, any one of the many which Homœopathy can present for its mode of treatment, our opponents might have some show of scientific foundation. But it does not possess a single support, offered by any law of nature, for the justification of its Therapeutics; it gives itself no trouble, moreover, about such a possession and continues to heal its patients at random. One ought to possess a shadow of science at least, in order to be able to give any *account* of his doings. In no branch of natural science, in no domain of human affairs, do men act so utterly without any point of support, going upon faith and trust, and the assertions of others, as in physiological medicine. This ignorance, however, does not prevent it from refusing to recognize Homœopathy, for it never acknowledges the possibility that there can be any knowledge higher than its own. Such arrogance must be met by the remark, that, as is well known, the advance in science is first made by this, that the most learned feel that they always know less than they desire.

How long the tormented public must still suffer, as martyrs for the grade of knowledge forced upon it by our opponents, can not under prevailing circumstances, be foreseen.

In closing this paragraph, I feel the necessity of presenting also, the deductive form of conclusion, since ignorance of it may be observed in many learned men. One might suppose that it would be easy to deduce the confirmation of an assertion from facts actually observed in regard to it.

If I affirm for example, that the Great Bear revolves around the

polar star, because daily observation teaches it, or, if an adherent
of physiological medicine maintains that he performed a cure, because his patient really recovered from his disease, both affirmations
lack the addition of the causes or conditions, owing to which those facts
might be possible. For, the necessity of that which actually has passed
before us, is by no means proven by such assertions: hence they. are
all without value. The cause which makes it necessary, however, that
we see the Great Bear revolve around the North Pole, is the motion of
our earth, which only exact experiments and observations teach, and,
among the conditions which give us an insight into the necessary course
of a cure by art, above all, belongs the knowledge of the causes, the
drug provings, which must previously be established by experiment
and observation.

Hence, in order to attain to a confirmation of an assertion by observed facts, we need three operations of reasoning. The first operation consists in the results of experiments and observations made with
regard to therapeutics, thus in the results of drug provings. The
second operation consists in the conclusions based upon the laws of
nutrition, in connection with the law of similarity, according to previous paragraphs. The third operation is the test by new experiments
and observations upon the sick, by which the conclusions of the
second operation are verified or overthrown.

In this wise, only, confirmatory conclusions from the effect to the
cause are possible. Thus, in the first and second operations, *known*
quantities must be given in order to find out the third which is *unknown*,
a result which, in consequence, is 'infallible. Hence nothing can be
scientifically confirmed, which can not be referred back to law, and the
conditions of which can not be given.

Since the physicians of physiological medicine know nothing of
deductive conclusions, they naturally always fall into fallacies, partly
on account of their inconsiderate assertions, about the cures effected
by them, partly on account of their silly affirmations about the impossibility of Homœopathic cures.

§ 90.

It is remarkable, with regard to the history of all natural sciences,
during our century, how the opponents of Homœopathy have, for more
than half a century, waged a bitter war, without knowing that they
were contending against relative ideas without meaning, and to this

very day, we see the most distinguished scholars using the most fabulous stratagems in order to attack the doctrine of the *simile*.

They are all easily thrown overboard if one does not inconsiderately dispense with the guide of category.

An opponent of Homœopathy says, for example, that Homœopathic medicine tastes of nothing but alcohol, hence can not have any virtue. This is merely a conclusion from the quality, which can easily be made to look ridiculous by use of the other categories. Besides, many infusoria form their iron coats of mail in water which does not taste of iron, nor can chemistry discern therein the least trace of this metal.

Another simply declares, " I don't believe, once for all, that Homœopathy can produce a cure." That again is an opinion merely from the category of modality and may be overthrown by the other categories, as well as by the scheme of modality itself. The *bon mot* of Buchner is so striking that I must quote it ; he replied to such an affirmation : " The ox does not believe it either, and yet is cured." The adherents of Homœopathy are increasing also among the farmers. Even at the famous Prussian stud, Trakhenen, the veterinary surgeons are Homœopaths, and certainly the government is not given to trust such expensive animals to any doubtful treatment. Man seems to be held at a lower value.

A third tells you that a child ate up a whole case of Homœopathic medicines, without the least harm, hence these medicines can't do any good. That is a false conclusion from the category of relation and finds its confutation in itself, since, for this very reason, the homœopathic remedies are thus prepared, that they shall do no injury to the *parts remaining sound*; for, without the help of these, the sick parts can not be made well. On the same ground of relation, they might say that Hepar Sulphur. would not cure a well child of croup ; for where there is nothing, there even the emperor has lost his rights.

§ 91.

Another one adds, " Since every patient and every hospital can be supplied with Homœopathic drugs at 90 per ct. less than the allopathic, the allopathic druggists can no longer make a living, which ought not to be." It is true, indeed, that very many druggists are the most violent opponents of Homœopathy. That objection, however, only arises from private interests. All the whale fishers in London objected, in vain, against lighting the city by gas and, without obtaining the desired result. Charles I., in 1634, had a sawmill, propelled by wind, torn down, because it took the bread away from the laborers.

Such things can happen, even in these times, as may be seen in the Allgemeine Homœopathische Zeitung Nos. 5 and 6 (for 1861) in a letter from Bavaria.

In Bavaria, the preparation of Homœopathic remedies has lately, been allowed, even to allopathic apothecaries, because Homœopathy is not represented in circles which have the control over these matters.

In consequence of some disputes naturally arisen from such an unnatural state of affairs, a homœopathic physician, residing in a place where there is no homœopathic pharmacy, received from his magistrate the draft of an official paper, the contents of which were as follows, viz. that he, the physician in question, should only have the right of dispensing the prescribed remedy of a higher potency if,1. The druggist H, should refuse to prepare the drug thus ordered, and 2. *in case of refusal*, the Dr. must satisfy the magistrate that he had the skill and knowledge necessary for the very peculiar preparation of the high potencies.

Thus, from a graduated physician, who must have graduated in Pharmacy as well, such evidence was still deemed necessary; not however from the apothecary and his clerks!

Now that druggist refused that physician the prescribed preparation of a high potency and the physician presented the evidence required by the official documents on the 5th of October. Not till October 12th, so long at least, the patient had to wait, he received another official document according to which, the evidence tendered by him was not considered sufficient and satisfactory.

But this judicial physician is an allopath; thus we have accuser and judge in one and the same person.

To put this matter in the right light, I need only to say that the preparation of homœopathic attenuations and high potencies is such a simple matter that, often in Hospitals, it is left to the Sisters of Mercy and Deaconesses, who, as I have had personal opportunity to satisfy myself, perform this office so carefully that no apothecary could do it any better, even if he were willing to do it at all.

For instance, the crude material, the vegetable tinctures, the preparations of animal substances, the earths, metals, &c. are always obtained from the homœopathic pharmacists, and from these substances

the attenuations and high potencies are made according to the prescription, by the physician or by the Sisters above named, according to
a two-fold scale. According to one, for the preparation of the first attenuation, a drop of the vegetable tincture is taken, or of the animal
preparation, and added to 99 drops of alcohol: from these 100 drops,
one drop is taken, and added to other 99 drops of alcohol, this makes
the second attenuation, &c.: on the other scale we add 10 drops of the
same preparation to 90 of alcohol, &c. Metals, and all substances, not
soluble in alcohol or water, are triturated with sugar of milk, in a
mortar, one grain to 99, or 10 to 90, according to the scale. But, after
the fourth trituration, we prepare the fifth attenuation or potency by
adding a grain of the drug, attenuated in the sugar of milk, to 100 drops
of alcohol. When these attenuations are carried up to the 30th or
higher, they are called the high potencies—certainly a process—part of
which is the shaking of each attenuation—which is not difficult for any
one to learn, but which a graduated physician is not permitted to undertake unless he has deposited evidence of possessing the necessary
skill and knowledge for its performance : evidence, moreover, which
will not be accepted, and by whom ? by one not versed in Homœopathy, though all other technical and scientific questions are allowed to
be decided by none but experts.

While Homœopathic physicians are recognized as practitioners
and the sick are entrusted to their care, they are deprived of 'the
means to fulfil their calling—a situation resembling that of a regi-
ment of soldiers which is expected to do fighting, but is given, for
this purpose, worthless weapons, or none at all, or is forbidden to
make use of those in its possession. On the other hand, the question
might be asked, by way of analogy, whether an enemy was ever called
upon to forge weapons, to be used against himself.

In Austria, they learned how to correct such abuses by the establishment of Homœopathic Faculties, and, if juries exist for the purpose of
trying the accused by his peers, why, then, should not homœopathic
physicians be judges in their own science, and their own affairs, instead
of their open enemies and opponents, who neither understand, nor
wish to understand, any thing of these matters ?

In brief, I should like to see that person who can find, in such
measures, any but partisan ends, in the interest of a special trade,
against the interest of the entire public.

But that was not all ! The above named physician finally received the following verbal declaration from the police, " *You shall dispense no drugs, not even if you can save life thereby.*"

Hence, *Dum ego salvus sim, pereat mundus* ?

Are then Apothecaries appointed to save life ? are the technical assistants to be set over the master, and does the welfare of the patient, really press more heavily upon the heart and mind of the apothecaries than of the physician, since the former is so tenderly cared for in preference to the physician ?

In this case, is it the physician only—if he is to be reduced to the rank of the Pariah, at all hazards—who is thus annoyed and not much more the public ?

The answer I leave confidently to the interested public, especially to the legal portion thereof. (Vide; Ein Wort ueber die in Frage gestellte Dispensirfreiheit der homœopathischen Aerzte, von Dr. juris F. G. Eckenberg, Coethen bei Gocht. 1860, or "Der moderne Laokoon" Leipzig, Purfurst. 1861.)

§ 92.

It is further asserted from the Category of modality that Homœopathy leads to quackery. To this may be replied, that, in the physiological school, the elements for such an evil abound much more, since its cures are conducted without law or order, merely by ear. According to the category of relation, this imputation, also, presupposes a very stupid public.

Another reproach brought up against Homœopathy is that it makes itself too popular, so that, at last, every body will be able to cure himself. I think it should be the final object of all science to know that it does not exist for its own benefit alone. This reproach, however, may in the mean time be considered as having been restricted to its proper limits by the foregoing pages, from which it can no longer be a matter of doubt whether ordinary knowledge suffices for the scientific practice of Homœopathy. Moreover, this reproach seems rather to be founded upon the self-felt insufficiency of our opponents, whose curative means lie so close together, and the use of which is so easy to grasp, that the apothecary's clerks run an opposition against allopathic physicians, more and more successful, every day.

It is true, Homœopathy can acquaint laymen with the laws of nature, in obedience to which its therapeutics is practised: it can not only teach laymen so much that they may know how to prescribe well in

the beginning of almost any disease until the physician, who often has
to be brought from a great distance, can reach the patient ; an advantage which the country resident, far from the city, knows how to prize;
but it does this very thing intentionally. Nevertheless, it does not,
in the least, fear the competition of non-professionalists, and its great-
ness and superiority, is manifest to every one in this, that it puts the
programme of its knowledge into the hand of the laity without fear of
competition; on the contrary, in the consciousness that confidence in
any matter can only arise from an understanding thereof. Thereby it
proves, at the same time, that it refuses every opportunity to deal in
quackery and mystery.

Thus all the charges against Homœopathy amount to nothing, just
as the above do : they are like light bodies which our opponents, with
a more than human outlay of power. seek every moment, to thrust at
Homœopathy, but without gaining their end.

The Law of Similarity Among our Opponents.

§ 93.

It is very clear that the *Simile* begins to haunt Allopathic physicians not a little, but they do not quite know whether what they see, in
the distance, is a mountain or a cloud.

At a full meeting of the members of the Medical Faculty of Vienna,
Nov. 14th, 1859, the essayist, during a debate on Syphilis between the
mercurialists and anti-mercurialists, mentioned Iodide of Potassium,
introduced into practice by Walase. and, while speaking of its advan-
tages and disadvantages, searched for the cause of the ever-recurring
strife in its very object; i.e. in the "*similarity*" existing between the
form of many syphilitic and mercurial affections. He maintained,
moreover, that the main point for the solution of this Gordian knot,
lay solely in the establishment of the "*differential diagnosis*" between
syphilis and mercurialism.

The art of observation in Therapeutics was never fallen so low.
Difference is the result of a subtraction. But for subtraction, we
can use no equivalent quantities which completely neutralize each
other. The school, however, gives as much quicksilver in Syphilis as
this disease needs to produce phenomena equivalent to mercurialism,
by which all difference is removed.

In this school, not only in Syphilis, but, generally, in all diseases,
such quantities of drugs are given, that a differential diagnosis between

the phenomena belonging to the disease and those which owe their origin to the injurious effects of the drugs prescribed, is absolutely impossible.

· Homœopathy, on the contrary, true to its principles, gives no remedy in such quantities as can generally produce real aggravation. Hence, if any aggravation is observed, which does not lie in the circle of the effects of the drug administered, and no improvement, the phenomenon is always owing to the morbific cause. Herein is contained the whole art of this differential diagnosis, which, for the school, is necessarily a Gordian knot and always must be. When such aggravations appear, however, in the circle of the effects of the remedy given, they serve Homœopathy as a confirmation that the indication was rightly made ; they are never injurious, and cease when the dose is diminished.

§ 94.

Thus Homœopathy discovered by *exact, deductive observations at the sick-bed*, possible to itself alone, still other things incomprehensible to its opponents. It is careful even with its minute dose, and, in many cases, especially the chronic, it avoids repetition thereof, on the ground of the *law of immunity* which also is known to it alone.

It is an old experience in Homœopathy that the consequences of mercurialism, iodism, &c. produced by large allopathic doses, are perfectly cured, and, often, in a short time, with the high homœopathic attenuations of the same substances, mercurius, iodine, &c.

These, scientifically expressed, are cures according to the law of repulsion of likes, in which way manifold immunities against various morbid causes may be produced. This holds good especially with regard to morbific causes from matter which belongs to the fundamental substances of nature, of which the organism is composed and which are most abundantly diffused in the organism, such as Oxygen, Carbon, Nitrogen, Hydrogen, Sulphur, Phosphorus, &c., or from organic substances and also from many function-remedies, according to the capacity of the organism to be saturated with them.

Hitherto, it has always remained a secret, how the snake catchers protected themselves against the bites of poisonous serpents. All we know is, that they take something, that makes them deadly sick, and sometimes actually kills them : that each one wants to have to do with only one species of snake and no other. Sometimes they are as inexperienced, as many arsenic-eaters, and take too much or too often of it. At other times, they can, owing to natural laws, produce no immunity against the results of the serpent's bite in any other way than by getting used to it, as laymen say, i.e. by gradually saturating the organism with it. But there are some poisons to which the organism can not become accustomed, i.e. the faculty of producing immunity against external influences, depends upon the quantity, quality and relation of such substances to the organism.

Thus the laws of nature tell us what we can not perceive by the medium of the senses.

From my own experience, I know that the men and women working in gun-cap factories, in which gases containing prussic acid are given off, gain entire immunity against cholera, which, according to Homœopathic drug-provings, we know to be a poisoning by prussic acid, arising from a negative electric condition of the atmosphere. On the other hand, the women become barren.

In brief, this law of immunity taught Homœopathy, not only that many drugs should be given in minute doses but, often, also, in a single dose only, in order to allow it to act till a pause in the curative process has manifested itself.

Homœopathy has hit upon this law by its practice with the *Simile*, consequently it is its lawful property. Besides, it has still another signification.

It often happens, for example, in the administration of Homœopathic remedies, that the medicine, though strictly indicated, and given according to the *Simile*, suddenly ceases to act. This occurs as soon as the parts which are not diseased become super-saturated. Herein, at the same time, lies the reason of the Homœopathic rule, not to repeat the dose without cause.

There is scarcely a homœopathic law of nature which is more readily accessible to experiment, than that of immunity, to convince the opponents of homœopathy of the necessity of high homœopathic potencies in many cases.

If, however, any one speaks of such phenomena based upon natural law, to an adherent of the physiological school, he laughs at it in his unbelief, although his attention ought to have been called to this point by vaccination, the result of which, from the smallest dose, we have to wait for from eight to ten days. However, one can not expect him to understand a language that he never learned, still less such a comprehensive science as Homœopathy. However, I shall offer him an opportunity easily to convince himself of the truth of my remarks. Let him give to a sycotic patient, (and many Leucæmic patients belong to this class, of whom he must have heard something at least from Virchow,) let him give Thuja 30, just *once*, and observe awhile the phenomena which will present themselves in his patient. But, previously, he must have learned how to guard against optical delusions, in the same way as the beginner with the microscope does.

§ 95.

Even in the most abominable recent excesses of physiological medicine, in the utterly superfluous syphilization, we hear of the "similarity,, which is said to exist between syphilis and the product from the inoculation of the syphilitic secretions. Dr. Kalischer—Die Syphilization, Berlin, 1860—says furthermore "that by syphilisation the *principle* is established that a poison can be entirely destroyed by itself and driven out of the organism." Here, consequently, perceived facts are made to pass for principles. One must confess, that these gentlemen make easy work in explaining matters.

But principles are fundamental laws of Nature and what is the name of this principle according to which the *constant course* of events in syphilization may be explained? But this course is not even constant since, in many cases, the inoculation is quite without results. Both as regards the conditions of this want of results and the naming of that principle, our opponents, if they wish to know them, must condescend to inquire of Homœopathy: they will there obtain correct information.

This polemic pamphlet among the opponents of Homœopathy, some of whom aver that syphilization wars against *sound reason*, contains many things, which for their deportment towards Homœopathy, they might remember with profit. For example, " one does not wish to experiment with something that wars against sound reason, nay, not even to see the experiments of others, upon learning what nonsense they lead to, and if one be compelled, even, to concede that the results of syphilization were really well established facts, he is inclined to explain them differently. The possibility is, for instance, presumed, that syphilitic diseases had disappeared on account of a well regulated diet, a good bed, &c."

However, their ignorance prevents them from thinking of the law

of immunity, the property and discovery of Homœopathy, in accordance to which, the processes of these inoculations must run their
course and find their explanation.

It is no wonder in blind man's buff, that the catcher tries for all
the children without catching any one; but when the same happens to
learned professors with eyes unbound, then it becomes really too
ridiculous.

The reason these gentlemen suddenly stand helpless, at the intro-
duction of these discovered similarities, as if a star which they had not
been used to see, were all at once dazzling their sight, lies in the
difference between the two kinds of general ideas, between perception
and law. Any man can, from any event, form an idea which may suit
him. But that idea has only subjective value, so long as the objective
law, pertaining thereto, has not been found.

As, however, the perception of the real remains without necessity,
so the law itself remains without reality. Hence, each must, as regards
the knowledge which is to make up a science, complement each other,
and thus the gentlemen know very well the reality of what has been
perceived, but lack the proof of the necessity of that which is real;
hence, they have no science. Chemistry, for example, is no science, as
yet; it is only an empiricism, a collection of experiments. Not till the
new theory of types and the spectral analysis appeared, did we catch
the light of the distant ray which promises a final passage from the
dark shaft into daylight. Yet it had the effrontery to arrogate to itself
inferences with regard to the science of Homœopathy, as an angry
man does about an object still hidden, yet very unpleasant to him in its
foreboding.

Abstract Philosophy Among our Opponents and their Opinions about their own Therapeutics.

§ 96.

To show that these assertions are not of my seeking, and that I
have only so far directed them against individuals as these individuals
are naturally responsible for their own expression, to show, moreover,
that the teachers of the physiological school have quite lost their way
as regards the admissibility of data offerred for the explanation of natural phenomena, it would be easy to write volumes.

Instead of that, I will add a few more examples, of recent date, from the prize essay upon the laws of the carnivora, by Drs. Bischoff and Voit, published in 1860.

This treatise does not bring anything new to light, and its only importance consists in this, that it merely confirms things already known, and corrects an error in calculation, previously made, concerning the significance of water as an equalizer in the organism : this significance of water, however, could or should have been known to them, as it was to me, and as is evident from my above quoted work, which appeared months before their experiments : for before one experiments, he ought at least to know from *one* part of the experiment, *wherewith* he can and will experiment.

In the preface to this treatise we are given to understand, among other things, that only from the *molecular forces* which announce themselves by *attraction* or *pressure, effects of motion* and *effects of heat* are deduced as *manifestations of forces.*

Here we have a list of qualities served up, quite devoid of any subjective idea; without any object to which they could be referred—hence a mere opinion.

That is the method of the old abstract philosophy, which sought entirely to free reflexion from the senses, but long ago proved a perfect failure.

There are no effects of motion and effects of heat without objects, but only quantities of motion and degrees of heat, which can even be brought about in a body by an external cause acting thereupon.

Neither can, from molecular forces, any other forces be inferred, for no quality can be deduced from, or explained by, another.

Moreover, the molecular forces can not make themselves known, for they are themselves the manifestation of the action of a cause upon their material molecules ; these only can make their existence known, by their forces, whenever they find opportunity for so doing, by the presence and property of some other substances.

Finally, the assertion that molecular forces operate by attraction or pressure, is false, for the same reason; it is an opinion, moreover, which is simply copied from Liebig. The molecules affect other molecules self-actingly—they are living : they manifest their forces either in the form of the attraction of unlikes or in that of repulsion of likes, and then, in both cases, either by contact or at a distance.

As regards these molecular forces, which, according to *Liebig* and

Bischoff, act independently and by virtue of their own inherent powers, by attraction or pressure, the best study of them is presented by the Cramer Klatt wire tack machine ; a pull and a pressure, and the tack, finished and complete, drops from the machine, which however, does but a part of all this, for the motion of its members is owing to the steam power.

Truly one is led to think that Liebig is right after all, for Homœopathy is justified in deriding such degrees of perception.

§ 57.

Another sentence in this treatise of Bischoff asserts "that the effect of a force does not change, so long as the state of the matter, with which the force is connected, and to which it owes the arrangement of its molecules, is not changed."

In the first place " the force " is not connected with "the state of the matter," but is dependent upon it, and, moreover, the matter does not owe the arrangement of its molecules to the force, but just exactly the reverse, since by force nothing else can ever be understood, than the property of a body proceeding from the arrangement and quality of its molecules.

In the days of a Keppler or a Newton, one would have blushed to appear in public with an essay of such contents.

Since in the moment of perception, but one scheme is given, that of the modality of the occurences, in the moment of thought, however, the three others are presented, yet the act of thinking, with the opponents of Homœopathy, as has just been shown, is only an individual, sometimes, indeed, an involuntary mode, of perception ; it naturally remains to them a riddle how Homœopathy, (to which they impute the same individual perceptive mode, for they know no other, and hence indulge themselves in drawing conclusions from themselves relative to Homœopathy), can attain to necessary truths.

Herein, as the reader will have already noticed, lies, at least as far as science is concerned, the *chief reason* of the persecutions which our opponents have carried on against Homœopathy. Homœopathy therefore, is not the cause of these persecutions, but our opponents themselves bear the whole responsibility with their inferior state of knowledge. Moreover the possibility of such persecutions lies, not in Homœopathy, but in the *despotic power* of the majority, from which every science should remain unmolested.

To complete the comparison betwen Allopathy and Homœopathy, it remains, now, that I should give, as briefly as may be, the present stand point of this majority in its own word. For this purpose, I quote the leading article in the opening of the recently begun Zeitschrift fuer Hygienie, medizinische Statistik and Sanitatspolizei, by Oesterlen, taken from a favorable criticism of the same in Vol. ii. of the Prager Vierteljahrsschrift, 1860.

In the first place, the idea is emphasized in this paper "that the cultivation of *Hygiene* (hence the science of health) may bring about a better future for therapeutics." Thus Oesterlen positively thinks, just as Virchow does with regard to Biology, that, from health, § 21, some conclusion as to a remedy may be possible. Alas! what premises will not be searched by the opponents of Homœopathy in their blind efforts for a therapeia! Indeed, every imaginable one except Homœopathy, where such a therapeia can be found!

" For," he continues, " so long as there was no science, no statistics, one could satisfy himself and others with illusions, and when Quetelet presented the axiom that the healing art exercised but little influence upon the death rate, we can understand why practice did not always consider that it was under great obligations to statistics."

Thereby, of course, the practice of that majority is understood. Besides, science and statistics are made, here, synonomous.

We may, it is true, call statistics an empirical science, a science of riddles, the solution of which, however, it denies us; for if, for example, in this year, so and so many eggs were eaten in Paris, and in another year again another number, which would amount to a specified sum in ten or 100 years, who will tell us the causes and consequences thereof? To put statistical questions to nature is indeed the least that can be done in natural science, for it does not give us an answer to such questions. Bacon said we should question nature, and, by the *art of experiment and of observation* seek her answer. *Empiric* sciences spring, as a rule, only from the senses, *rational* sciences from these and reason. All our knowledge it is true, begins with empiricism, with the enumeration of similar cases, §10; but all our knowledge does not arise from empiricism, but also from the connection of empiric perceptions according to natural laws.

" Now," Oesterlen proceeds, " the main results in statistics may be comprised in the following propositions. 1. Diseases, epidemics, untimely death are the simple and necessary consequences of our manner of our living. 2. The insufficient fulfilment of the relations of life (the conditions of life would be a better expression in both places, v. G.) is the determining cause of all diseases. 3. Having once originated, diseases run their course according to fixed laws and with the • same inward necessity from which they originated (where does the outward necessity remain, v. G.) ; on which account it is but seldom that human art can effect any essential change."

That encourages the conceit that all medical skill and knowledge reside in Allopathy alone : any one who is ignorant of those laws given in § 11, naturally enough, can not imagine an art and science of healing.

"In living bodies, there are no isolated states; the usual levers and mechanisms of life are herein activity only variable in their direction and results; the latter are the effect of very few natural causes, among which the unfavorable condition of all the relations of life, wants and mistakes of every kind are by far the most significant. With its scientification, medicine has *almost ceased to believe in the absolute power of making the sick well, as it can no longer believe in miracles.*

Virchow's prophecy that he would see a rational Therapeia arise from biology and ætiology, § 43, has thus not been fulfilled, and what was Therapeutics quite recently and previous to its scientification by means of its latest statistics ? If statistics occupies the lowest position of empiricism, since thousands and millions of similar events can never hit upon any of their causes or laws, what then have physicians, occupying such a position, thus far practiced. No other answer can be given than, Quackery, and what must they practice now ? I should hardly have ventured to draw, by such sharp outlines, the infirmity and therapeutic incapacity of allopathy or physiological medicine, as it has done itself in those words.

§ 99.

This great distrust with which physiological medicine, in a painful manner finds itself compelled to meet its own therapeutics, and the Nihilism at which it has, in consequence thereof, arrived, depend, according to what has already been said, upon the error of teleologically considering the natural events in and upon the organism, as if they were works of human hands ; that, hence, it directs its aid for the diseased organism, now to regulate its forms and now its functions, as if it had a work of art to repair, and not a product of nature, before its eyes.

However, *the identity of the master, of the work and the material is the characteristic feature of a product of nature; the diversity of all three, that of a product of art.*

Since, most unfortunately, it has had the good luck, now and then, to maltreat the organism in this direction, with success, as especially its emetics, purgatives and narcotics very rarely fail in the effect aimed at, it boldly infers, though without any scientific foundation whatever, that a disease may be treated like a chemical preparation, a piece of meat or some blood. It has merely imaginary aims, in accordance with which prescriptions must be made for the organism.

Yet it is a fruitless therapeutic labor to devise, for the operation of the organism, an object foreign to it and to adjust to it remedies in order to remodel one of its substances or to lead and compel a function to something else than that which suits it.

In order to understand the working of nature, we must not only make comparisons with the work done in laboratories or other workshops of art, but must watch it also in its own workshops, as is done by the Homœopathic drug provings, for then nature will not only answer, but will also be our polar star.

The truth, and, indeed, even the thought of it, is quite strange to physiological medicine, that every thing in the organism has a mutual bearing, that it resists every strange substance, form, and function, which may be thrust upon it, against its own laws, and, when this ceases to be the case, that then it succumbs to this unnatural violence, wholly or in part. Whoever does not know the laws which govern life, to him, of course, life can only be a miracle, and a cure from any disease, must consequently seem a still greater, an *unheard of miracle*.

But we read further, "The fall of a groschen in the price of bread, a new branch of industry, a good building law, technical improvements in houses and cities, drains and sewers &c., appear, to medicine, perhaps, as very small matters, lying quite remote from its lofty aim of saving man; and yet thereby is certainly done more to create and preserve health and life, than by its entire healing art."

Yet, has the healing art nothing to do but to preserve and create health and life? That is the duty of its smallest portion, ætiology and prophylaxis; it has mainly to cure the sick, and, for this purpose, has its own art and science.

In conclusion, we give the following sentence from this leading article. "While the intelligent physician, in the consciousness of the limits of his power, is *at the same time* the most modest, it is unendurable to the *empiric* to be unable to cure or explain anything."

Modesty is the honest acknowledgement of mediocrity; the profession of Allopathy may plume themselves therein. Homœopathy has no use for such people.

An empiric, moreover, not only does not know how to explain any thing, he does not even wish to explain anything; quite different it is with a man possessed of a theoretically and practically formed science; but this science has been lost in physiological medicine.

These few sentences, from the present times, give a true picture of the present standpoint of physiological medicine, drawn by itself. What now, in view of this great retreat from a therapeutics, inaccessible and hence imaginary, back to Hygiene, statistics and the police, will the allopathic apothecaries say, and what *ethical* significance, belongs to the prescriptions which nevertheless find their way to their shops every day?

Points of Attack Against Homœopathy,

§ 100.

In conclusion, I shall afford to the exalted wisdom of our opponents the pleasure of seeing disclosed the weak point of homœopathy existing to this very day.

It is the word "Homœopathy" itself, together with the "Similar" in the Hahnemannian motto, as regards its variablity for the formation of conclusions.

Upon this point they may direct their attacks as long as it gives them any pleasure.

There are, in every language, ideas which do not arise from experience and perception, but from the reflections of reason. To these belong to the ideas of sameness, difference, similarity, contrast, &c.

Such reflective ideas do not serve for the definition of an object, but, only, for the indication of a relation, for the definition of this or that comparison under the predominance of subjective ideas. Such inaccurate forms of comparison, in daily use, belong, of course, to the analytical instruments by which conclusions may be formed by syn-. thesis with experience. Hence, the simile, as Hahnemann phrased it, is a proposition which cannot maintain itself against the most shallow assertions of its opponents.

But few men know what harm may arise when one is too little objective in his manner of expression and makes assertions by the use of relative ideas which contain no real, but only an apparent meaning.

Full opportunity is given to every opposition to attack, in all directions, such defenceless ideas, a warfare by which unhappily, however, great truths are often concealed for centuries. The law of similarity is a striking example thereof.

For how the combination "Homœopathy" by means of that "homoion pathos," can express what is to be understood thereby, that is a Therapeutics, according to natural law, it is impossible to tell.

In the signification of new ideas, we are not permitted to vary from the natural agreement of all sciences regarding the expression of an idea, in order that thus all opportunity may be cut off from every body, to draw suppositions from such words suitable to individual fancy.

A word must form an equivalent for a whole explanation, about the meaning of which no one can be in doubt. Nothing finds its way more rapidly among men than that which, by a suitable choice of words, may be, nailed fast, as it were, to the memory.

Since, however, Hahnemann has attached to our opponents the nickname of allopathy, which is of a similar value, and they choose to use it to characterize themselves, to this very day, all mutual reproaches are superfluous.

The difference, even here consists in this, that Homœopathy, long ago, declared this name which Hahnemann gave it, unsuitable, and with this name, as with similar unsuitable expressions, for example, with the word "inflammation" it does not confound facts as does Allopathy, which, in every inflammation, thinks at once of the whole medicinal fire apparatus, of its famous *apparatum antiphlogisticum*, of its frightful vampyrism, and practices accordingly.

The Law of Similarity.
§ 101.

Having now sufficiently attended to our opponents, it remains, yet, briefly to present the manifold significations which have been attributed to the law of similarity, according to its extent and contents in the course of time and from the investigations made.

In the inquiry about the objects of the law of similarity, all four modes of perception which the human mind possesses, had to be called into requisition, the *mathematical*, the *empiric*, that of *mathematical abstract philosophy* and *logic* : we had always to consider, moreover, two different domains of life, the outer world, as well as the inner life.

Mathematical perception arises from the construction of ideas. Construction is only the presentation of an idea by the elaboration of a conception therewith. By construction, the idea gains its object, its form, as we gain the idea of a circle by the actual construction of its figure. The *forms*, the units of forms for the construction of objects, which stand under the idea of the law of similarity, we learned to know in a three-fold form ; once in the human organism, in its physiological, next in its spontaneous pathological state, for the third time in its pathological form, artificially produced by drug provings, according to definite laws.

To this also belongs the established law of dose, according to the law of similarity, in relation to its quantity according to natural law. Thus justice was done to the category of the *Quantity* of the law of similarity.

In the second, in *empiric* relation, the necessary quality of the Homœopathic drug and its dose is set forth, and, both the spontaneous and the artificially produced objects of comparison from empiric perception for homœopathic diagnosis, indication and prognosis, were subordinated to the law of similarity, hence, according to the category of its *quality*.

In the third regard, the relation of these quantitative and qualitative laws was brought into dependent connection with the natural laws of life and its nutrition and the course of the cure thereby explained, hence justice was done to the "curantur" according to the law of similarity upon the ground of the category of *relation*.

Finally, in the fourth regard, all these existences facts and events were recognized as *dependent upon* and *necessary* according to these natural laws, corresponding to the category of modality, and thus the validty of the former was established by the latter.

By this general subordination of these events and facts to the necessary laws of nature, and by their explanation according to their connection with these laws, the *theory* of Homœopathy is built up for all time.

§ 102.

Now, as regards the universal significance of the law of similarity, that conclusion, as is well known, the validity of which springs from these categories, together with its respective scheme, is a fundamental maxim or a *fundamental law* of nature, a principle upon which every thing in its sphere depends, and this character of the law of similarity effectively expresses by this thereby, that it is no object of sensual perception, but exists previous to every observation of the various past and future really therapeutic events in its sphere; because the conditions for its application, although a long while unknown, were always present and the law does not present itself by any motions, which, according to it, are wont to occur in course of a cure, any more than any other natural law, in course of the phenomena which happen in accordance therewith.

The *system* of Homœopathy thus announces itself from the perfect subjection of the particular to the principle and that which attains to the form of a perception by virtue of a principle, is a unit of perception in systematic form, consequently a science, and remains a science, a fact which no power in the world can change.

One part of the law of similarity, that of the presupposition according to natural law was more or less abstracted by Hahnemann just as Galileo even, not by experimemt, but by reflecting, hit upon the fundamental law of the relativity of all movements, and only its empiric part proceeded from induction. From logical abstractions, however, we obtain laws; from inductions, maxims, and since the former were never spoken of, the law of similarity, for a long time had only the validity of a *doctrine*.

From this sphere and the contents of the law of similarity it is finally evident that although it formed, as a doctrine for the therapeutic indication, a *rational* inventive maxim, it was yet, raised to a *law of nature*, only at the moment when its physiological and pathological bases were also found: consequenuty, the elements for the constant course, even of *material* movements, within the organism were given.

Conformable to these material relations, its formula was thus enlarged: " *The more two diseases, arising from different causes and conditions, agree with each other, the more certain is it that the one will be cured by the cause of the other.*

I hardly think it necessary to call attention to the fact that this formula perfectly expreses a conclusion according to the fundamental ideas of mathematical abstract philosophy, and comprises the contents of what has been set forth in this treatise : it is the deduction of a conclusion from other conclusions, hence a logical conclusion.

§ 103.

Finally, the form of conclusion of the law of similarity is the hypothetic-divisive and, as a hypothetical one, equal to the following : if we have two triangles, of various size, agreeing in form, their homologous sides are proportionate with each other. Its divisive form is therein contained, that it draws conclusions from the *parts* of its objects of comparison to the *whole* of the complete cure.

On the other hand the law of similarity is *no analytical proposition*, otherwise all physicians would long ago, and easily, have understood it. Yet every physician ought to possess scientific culture enough, to know that he can make no experience which contravenes an inductive doctrine, a rational induction, an abstract fundamenla law of nature, a natural law. But our opponents lack the perception for the perceptive and essential bases of the law of similarity, as many beings can not see the eagle floating far above them in the firmament.

All this our opponents can not understand. Hence the occurrence with them of the so-called *involuntary Homœopathy* which, without any reason for being and knowing, even in allopathy sometimes produces actual, though according to their indication, only accidental cures ; for they can always be explained and indeed *only* be explained by the law of similarity.

§ 104.

It surely requires great courage in defiance of the truth, to hold fast to errors disclosed and proven by facts and natural laws ; it is the courage of egoism, of traditions, of prejudice, of ignorance, of absolutism which, through the entire history of the human race, instead of meeting the truth with proof, met it with insults, injuries and sophisms and, finally stoned and crucified it.

This history, however, teaches us yet another courage, namely, to submit with resignation to the inevitable fate, that truth must first suffer crucifixion, before it can stand forth victor, a courage which under the weight of such vexations does not falter but grows in strength.

CONTENTS.

Open Letter to Prof· Justus v. Liebig, &c., &c.

INTRODUCTION.

		PAGE.
§ 1.	Hahnemann's Dogma,	1
§ 2.	Its Recognition and Rejection,	1
§ 3.	The Bases of both. The Indications of the Physiological school, or Allopathy in form of a Syllogism,	2
§ 4,	Inventive Maxims for the Discovery of the Law of Similarity, or of the Simile.	3
5.	Schleiden and Humboldt upon Mathematical Natural Philosophy,	3
§ 6.	Molleschott on Philosophy. Law ; Lower and Higher train of Thought, a priori, a posteriori,	4
§ 7.	Pre-suppositions for the Establishment of the Law of Similarity by Hahnemann,	6
§ 8.	Causal Law ; The Contrarium in its Effect upon the Simile of the Indication.	7
§ 9.	The Simile drawn from Induction and Abstraction,	7
§ 10.	The Inductive form of the Simile. Empiric and Rational Induction,	8

General Physiology.
§ 11.	Abstraction. Induction. Law. Fundamental law of nature,	9
§ 12.	Law of Causality and Reciprocal Action,	9
§ 13.	Law of Specification. Growth of the Cranial bones in infancy,	10
§ 14.	Law of the Constancy of Masses and Forces in Relation to the Organism and to the effect of the Remedy,	11
§ 15.	Law of Life,	11
§ 16.	Law of Attraction and Repulsion. Metamorphosis. Diosmosis. Localization of Matter in the Organism,	11
§ 17.	Matter and Forces. Process of Nature,	12
§ 18.	Hylotopics of the Organism,	12
§ 19.	Metabolics of Matter in the Organism.	12
§ 20.	Hylometrics of the Organism,	13
§ 21.	Law of Proportional Oscillation and Reproduction. Idea of Health. Crisis. Combinatory Method of studying Nature,	13
§ 22.	Law of Nutrition. Empiricism. Fact.	14

General Pathology·
§ 23.	Law of pathological Nutrition and Function. Idea of Disease,	15
§ 24.	Pathological Hylotopics and Metabolics,	15
§ 25.	Example, from Virchow's Cellular pathology, of Gout,-	16
§ 26.	Criticism of this example according to natural law.	16

83

§.27. Groups of Symptoms according to Individuality. Measles, Intermittent fever, - - - - - - - - 17

§ 28. Specific pathological form of every disease. Cause and Condition. Pathological object, - - - - - - - 17

§ 29. Bodily Constitution, and dependence of the group of symptoms thereupon, 18

§ 30. Permanent Morbid causes. Homœopathic Drug provings. Pathological hyloteretics (*vulgo* substitutions) and Metabolics. Antidotes. Succession of remedies, - - - - - - 18

§ 31. Sycosis. Psora. Rademacher. Substances favoring the action of hydrogen upon the blood and increasing the action of oxygen, - - 19

§ 32. Conclusions touching Hahnemann's Psora, and Virchow's Leucæmia. Opinion. Negation, - - - - - - 20

§ 33. Dyscrasiæ. Example from Virchow's Cellular Pathology, - - 21

§ 34. Chemistry, Microscopy, Dyscrasia, Atmosphere, Exhalation of Carbon by expiration. Intermittent fever, - - - - 21

§ 35. The blood as the bearer of permanent causes of consecutive changes, - 22

§ 36. Example to the point. Chlorosis. Substitution remedy. Homœopathic Drug provings for; the conclusions a priori and a'posteriori. Regressive Conclusions touching the Bodily Constitution from the above, and from the Indication. Method of Recognizing the Bodily Constitutions, - 23

§ 37. Relation of Immunity and Change in Disease, - - - 24

General Therapeutics.

§ 38. Cure by Art. Recovery. Curability. Incurability, - - - 24

§ 39. Cure in a way similar to the Disease. Cause of Cure, - - 25

§ 40. Organic Conditions for the completion of the Cure. Example from the blood cells, - - - - - - - 25

§ 41. Chemical, Microscopic Analysis, Chlorosis, Hydrocephalus. Essential Indication, - - - - - - - 26

§ 42. Object of Cure. Question touching the discovery of the drug, or, of the causes of the cure, - - - - - - 26

§ 43. Discovery of a rational Therapeia according to Virchow. - - 27

§ 44. Hahnemann's maxim for the Discovery of Remedies. The Art of Experiment. - - - - - - - 27

§ 45, Diseases Artificially Produced by drug-provings, - - - 28

§ 46. Example to the point from Virchow's Cellular Pathology. Salts of Silver, 28

§ 47. Authority and Tradition as the Motive of physiological Medicine for the use of Remedies, - - - - - - 29

§ 48, Metastasis according to Virchow. The Confounding this with processes of Nature according to the Laws of the lower train of thought, - - 29

§ 49. Artificially produced pathological Hylotopia by the drug proving with Benzoic acid. - - - - - - - 30

§ 50. Function Remedy. Allopathic Drug Doses, - - - - 30

§ 51. The Mode of Action of Function Remedy. Agens and Patiens, - 31

§ 52. Aconite. Phosphorus. Curative process according to the Laws of Nature. Its value, - , - - - - - - 31

§ 53. The Analytic and Synthetic Comparison. Units of Comparison. The Mode of Establishing Homœopathic Indications, - - - 32

§ 54. The Contraria Contrariis Curantur as the Indication of Physiological Medcine, - - - - - - - 32

§ 55. The Analytic Comparison of Physiological Medicine for the Establishment of the Indication. Example, Gout, - - - 33

§ 56. The Natural Law of the Contrarium of the Indication. The Mode of Establishing the Indication in Gout by Physiological Medicine, , - 34

§ 57. Proving of Colchicum. Differential Diagnosis between Gout and Rheumatism, - - - - - - - 35

§ 58. Differential Diagnosis between two Spontaneous Diseases as understood by Allopathy not needed in Homœopathy, - - - - 35

§ 59. The Regard given to accompanying circumstances in making out the Homœopathic Indication. Byronia, Rhus, Law of Equipoise of rest and motion. Crisis, - - - - - - - - 36

§ 60. Curative Method of Physiological Medicine in overpowering the function of parts remaining healthy. Functional Tension. Equipoise of rest and motion in the Organism as regards the Therapeutics of the Physiological school, - - - - - - - 37

§ 61. Experiences of Homœopathy, Law of the Remembrance and Expectation of Similar Cases. Therapeutic Schemes of Homœopathy, . - 38

§ 62. General and Special Therapeutics. Pedantry, - - - 38

§ 63, Homœopathic Examination of the Patient, - - - 39

§ 64. Diagnosis and Indication of Physiological Medicine. Intermittent fever, 40

§ 65. The same continued, - - - - - - - 40

§ 66. Authority in Homœopathy. The Empiric Rule of the Simile in Hahnemann's time. Rationality of Homœopathy, - - - - 41

§ 67. Idea of Proportion. Reciprocal Action. Causality, Opium, Panaritium, 41

§ 68. The Simile as a Guide to finding the Remedy, . - 43

§ 69. The Concomitant Circumstances, - - - - 43

§ 70. Conclusion of the Physiological School from the Result to the Cause, - 44

§ 71. Surgery and Midwifery, - - - - - . 45

§ 72. A Rational Therapeutics must make Calculations for all diseases to come, even those not yet known, - - - - - 46

§ 73. Drug provings of Physiological Medicine upon Animals. Conclusions therefrom, - - - - - - - - 47

Posology.

§ 74. The Fundamental Principle of the Relativity of all Motions contains the Law of the Dose according to the Simile, - - - 48

§ 75. The Quantity of the Dose is thus Determined by the Laws of Nutrition, 48

§ 76. Law of the Effect of the Superficies, . - - - 49

§ 77. The Morbid Cause and the Dose Imponderable, - - - 49

§ 78. Condensation Occurring in the Preparation of Attenuations, - - 50

§ 79. Jolly's Experiments, - - - - - - 50

§ 80. Zero point of Attenuations. The Vehicle, - - ; - 51

§ 81. Chemistry and Spectral Analysis, - - . - - 52

§ 82. Example from Intermittent Fever and Quinine. The Frugality of Nature, 53

§ 83. The Chemical Allegation against the possibility of the Efficiency of Homœopthic Attenuations as regards their Effect of the Saliva and Gastric juices upon them. The Controversial Strategy of our Opponents, - 54

§ 84. The use of Larger Doses by Homœopathy compared with the Motives of Allopathy in using the same, - - . - - 56

§ 85. Auscultation, Percussion, Microscopy, chemistry in Allopathy and Homœopathy, - - - - - - - - 57

§ 86. Example from Practical Microscopy. Impotence. Woman's Milk, - 57

§ 87. Difference between Homœopathic (and Allopathic) Diagnosis, Prognosis and Indication shown by a Practical Example. Allopathic Evasion, - 59

§ 88. Mode of Preparing Remedies in Homœopathy and Allopathy, - 60

§ 89. Deductive Confirmation of the Simile. Impossibility of a Deductive Conclusion under Allopathy, - - - - - 61

§ 90. Strife with Proportional Ideas. Unbelief Regarding Homœopathy. Trakehnen. Injurious Treatment of Homœopathic Pharmacists, - 62

§ 91. Pharmacists, - - - - - - - 63

§ 92. Reproach of Charlatanry and Popularity against Homœopathy, - 66

The Law of Similarity Among Its Opponents.

§ 93. The Simile in Allopathy. Differential Diagnosis between the Effects of the Cause of Disease and those of the Drug Impossible in Physiological Medicine. Its Existence in Homœopathy, - - - - 67

§ 94. The Repetition of the Dose a Matter of the Art of Observation. Law of Immunity. The Loss of Efficiency of the Remedy according to the Law of Immunity, - - - - - - - - 68

§ 95. Syphilization of Physiological Medicine, Efficiency, Necessity, Knowledge, 70

Abstract Philosophy Among our Opponents and their Opinions of their own Therapeutics.

§ 96. Nutrition of Carnivora according to Drs. Bischoff and Voit. Fallacies after the Manner of the Old Natural Philosophy, - - - - 71

§ 97. The same Continued. Force and Matter, Scheme of Perception and Thought. The Chief Ground of the Persecution of Homœopathy, - 73

§ 98. Prof. Oesterlen on Therapeutics. The so-called Empiric and Rational Knowledge. Statistics, - - . - - 74

§ 99. Teleological View of Nature by Physiological Medicine, Ethical Significance of their Prescriptions, - - - - 75

Points of Attack Against Homœopathy.

§ 100. Ideas of Reflection in Homœopathy. Composition of the Word Homœopathy, - . - - - - - - 77

The Law of Similarity.

§ 101. The Law of Similarity in its Comprehensiveness and Contents. Theory of Homœopathy, - - - - - - 78

§ 102. The Law of Similarity a Fundamental Law of Nature, partly Discovered by Abstraction. The System of Homœopathy as a Science. The Law of Similarity partly discovered by Induction; a Rational Maxim and Indication, - - - - - - - 79

§ 103. Of the Law of Similarity - - - - - - 80

§ 104. Conclusion. - - - - - . - - - 81